Brody's Guide to the College Admissions Essay

Brody's Guide to the College Admissions Essay

Jay Brody and Toby Stock

iUniverse, Inc.
New York Lincoln Shanghai

Brody's Guide to the College Admissions Essay

iUniverse books may be ordered through booksellers or by contacting:

iUniverse
2021 Pine Lake Road, Suite 100
Lincoln, NE 68512
www.iuniverse.com
1-800-Authors (1-800-288-4677)

ISBN-13: 978-0-595-35582-2 (pbk)
ISBN-13: 978-0-595-80066-7 (ebk)
ISBN-10: 0-595-35582-X (pbk)
ISBN-10: 0-595-80066-1 (ebk)

Printed in the United States of America

Contents

Introduction

The college essay is a strange, rare creature:

It's a one-time thing. Most students write college essays just once in the fall of their senior year of high school, and then never again. That means applicants (and often parents) come into this project completely unaware of what the task entails or requires, having never done anything like it before.

The college essay is terribly important. In a world where students sometimes write dozens of pages for each graded class, it can be startling to imagine a 500-word piece holding such sway over something as monumental as college admissions. Yet next to grades and test scores, the essay is the most relevant part of the college application. When admissions officers read the essays, they not only evaluate them for quality, but also form unconscious impressions about the candidate: "Is this a likable person? Does he or she sound intelligent? Curious? Passionate?" Most important: "Do we want this person at our school?"

You can use all of the time and resources you need. Perhaps the best part about writing the college essay is this: despite all the stress and hubbub that surrounds the admissions process, students can write at their own pace. The essay isn't timed, and it isn't a pop quiz. Applicants have at least three months (and in reality much more time) to conceive, plan, and write a one to two-page paper. There's also plenty of time for students to show their essay to parents and teachers, to rethink, to revise, and generally to make all of the improvements that good writing requires.

About This Guide

At Brody Admissions (come visit us at www.brody.com!), we have guided hundreds of clients and families through the admissions process. And we finally decided to put all of our usual advice about the college essay into a book. That's what you're holding right now—our comprehensive guide to the college essay.

How does this guide differ from the other ones you'll find at the bookstore? Most strikingly, it's shorter—much shorter. That seemed to make the most sense. The meandering essay-writing manuals we have on our shelves are filled with mind-numbing detail, presumably intended to thicken each book enough to lend gravitas and an aura of authority. We left out the 15-point study plans and the six-page lesson on the use of commas; you'll find here only straightforward advice on what comprises a good admissions essay.

That said, participles shouldn't dangle and infinitives shouldn't be split. You need to make clean writing and good grammar a high priority. But if you're not a great writer, it may be easier to let a parent, teacher, or counselor catch such mistakes. We'll provide the basic rules about grammar, usage, and clear prose, and let you deal with the details. Our goal is simply to give you a short and effective lesson on how to brainstorm, plan, and write your essay.

Because we've cut out the fat, this guide is easy to use. And while it can hard to know what to do with a 200-page manual that includes all sorts of lessons, tasks, and rules, we know *exactly* what we expect you to do with our short and easy-to-read guide:

Read it cover to cover.

That's right. Now, or sometime soon, we want you to read this book straight through from beginning to end. It shouldn't take more than a few hours. While you can always go back to learn more about a particular issue, a careful once-through will ensure that you're properly approaching each stage of the essay-writing process.

Here's what's inside:

I. Know Your Audience. Who's reading these essays, anyway? What are they looking for?

II. Topics. What should I write about? Should I be serious or funny? What are some examples of good/bad topics?

III. Writing: Putting your Thoughts on Paper. Should I write it all at once? How much time should I leave? Do I need a dedicated workspace?

IV. Format, Structure, and Style. What should my essay look like? Formal or casual style? Is this more like a research paper or an editorial? Can I use incomplete sentences? Should I start with a famous quotation?

V. Writing Well. What are some good tips that will help me write well?

VI. Reviewing and Editing. How should I edit my essay? Should I show it to other people? Professionals?

VII. Successful Essays. Seven successful college essays, with complete reviews and notes about what works and what doesn't.

Let's get started.

1

Know Your Audience

You probably know from your English classes or, better yet, as a matter of common sense, that a writer always writes for a particular audience. A VCR instruction manual is written in a different style than a romance novel, which is absolutely nothing like an economics textbook (hopefully).

The most important reason these styles of writing are different is that they serve different purposes and different audiences. The guy setting up his VCR just wants to know how to understand the process and get each step over with as quickly as possible. The romance reader is looking to escape into a fantasy world. The economics student is trying to understand a complex subject.

You'll write the college essay for just one audience: the college admissions committee member. Who is this person who reads your essays and otherwise decides your fate? Well, that depends on where you're applying.

Top Schools

At today's most prestigious colleges (Harvard, Brown, Duke, Amherst, and so on), the people reading your essay are usually devoted admissions professionals. They use complex procedures to select applicants, and the essays are an important part of that process. Sure, the essays aren't *always* important. If you simply don't have the test scores and grades, you're not going to get in—busy admissions officers don't spend a lot of time reading essays from students who just aren't qualified. Similarly, on rare occasions a student will be so qualified or otherwise guaranteed admission that the essay just isn't important—unless the student writes something egregious, he or she will be admitted.

But for most applicants to top schools, essays will be read with a great deal of care. The person reading the essays is usually a tired, overworked admissions officer (sometimes working from home at night) who reads hundreds of essays each admissions season. With that much experience, the savvy admissions officer can get to the heart of your writing much more quickly than you'd expect.

Other Competitive Schools

What if you're *not* applying to a "top" school? Some schools require essays, and read them carefully, but are slightly less competitive than some of the names we've already mentioned. This includes a number of smaller schools with strong regional reputations. Most of the above rules still apply. The difference is that, while the profile of the admissions officer is likely still the same (a harried, experienced professional), the pool of competition may be a little less daunting.

This shouldn't change your strategy at all. You still need to produce stellar work, and take care of all of the other essay essentials we talk about later in this guide. Just be aware that your reader will be less inundated with powerful and perfect student essays. Standing out (for the sake of standing out) will probably be at less of a premium, and demonstrating your writing chops will be crucial.

Less Competitive Schools

Finally, there are some large state schools and local schools that don't have rigorous admissions requirements but still require an essay. Not surprisingly, the admissions process (and thus your audience) is a little different at those places. Often, an administrator or part-timer will be reading your essay (or sometimes, especially if your grades and test scores are too high or too low, *no one* will be reading it).

Make sure your essay looks well-written and solid to *any person* who might look it over. Don't write anything weird. Don't write anything too innovative or difficult to understand in a short time period. Write well and clearly, and cleanly answer the questions posed. At these schools, the essay is used more like GPAs and SATs than as a way to get to know you. The schools just want information about how well you write and how clearly you express your thoughts.

Writing for the Admissions Officers

Why is it important to know that someone who reads tons of these essays will evaluate yours? Why is it also important to know that, at least at the most competitive colleges, an intelligent admissions officer (often an alumnus of the school) is likely to be reviewing your application? It's important because you need to realize that *your final audience for the college admissions essay is not the same as the teachers and parents who tend to provide the most essay-writing advice.*

1. Admissions officers can smell insincerity from a mile away.

Because they read so many essays, these people are great at determining who's truly passionate about something and who's making it up. Writing about wanting to save the planet may sound great to your English teacher, who doesn't read these essays very often, but the admissions officer sees this all the time and it sounds phony. Unless you can back up what you say with real-life experiences, steer away from essay topics intended to make you sound benevolent or wise.

2. Admissions officers don't know you.

It's easy to forget that those helping you with your essays generally know you well. If you take a sarcastic tone in an essay, they're likely to be familiar with it. If you say something that could be construed as offensive, they know that deep down you're a good person. If you make a writing mistake, they remember that you're a great writer anyway.

Admissions officers, on the other hand, have never met you. This is probably the only thing they've ever read of yours, and they're only going to spend five to ten minutes at the most with your application. What they see is what you get. Be sure that the essay you write gets your message across *on its own*, without the need for any background or understanding of who you are.

3. Admissions officers have seen it all.

You probably can't come up with anything completely original. That essay where you pretend to be the family dog observing your life? The one that's a little weird but *so* clever? They've read that essay, so you get few or no points for originality.

More commonly, that essay about Outward Bound or visiting Africa is not going to be special *solely* because you had those experiences. You may not realize it, but a number of applicants to top colleges have done those things. So while they may have been transformative experiences for you, they don't mean much on their own to the admissions officers. Rather than rely on how special you are because of those experiences, explain why they were so meaningful to you (if you discuss them) and *have a point.*

4. Admissions officers have high standards

If you're one of the brighter kids at your school, you're probably one of the best writers there. English teachers are impressed by your papers. You don't make grammatical mistakes, and you understand how an essay should be put together. When your parents and teachers read an admissions essay on which you've spent a lot of time, they're bound to be impressed. And they'll tell you so.

Once that essay makes its way to Dartmouth or Northwestern, however, the landscape changes. Almost by definition, the schools where your essays really count are the ones where your competition is, on average, about as gifted as you are. Relatively speaking, you aren't a great writer anymore. In fact, even if your essay is well-received by friends and family, it's possible that it's actually *worse* than many of the essays of other top students from all over the country applying to the same school.

At the very least, you need to realize that your essay is most likely not going to blow anyone away. Don't become too comfortable in the praise of your readers, teachers, parents, and counselors. This isn't high school—college admissions is a competitive, national game and the judges (admissions officers) are playing by a new and tougher set of rules. Your essay should be the best thing you've ever written.

2

Topics

High school kids tell great stories. Why? While it's sometimes hard to realize at the time, life in high school is full of adventure and intrigue, as well as exploration and self-discovery. And as any family with only one phone line can attest, there's no shortage of things to talk about in the high school world. High school students spend hours each week on the phone, talking about everything and nothing. Hours more are spent chatting in school, after school, out on weekends, during the summer, and at just about every other opportunity.

So why, when it comes to finding something to write for a college application, does everyone seem to draw a blank? Why, almost every day during the fall application season, do intelligent 17 year-olds insist that they suddenly have absolutely nothing to talk about?

Because as a high school student, you don't—and shouldn't—have any clue about what makes a good college admissions essay.

A college admissions essay isn't like a science paper, a book report, a history essay, or anything else you've been taught to write. Frankly, a good college admissions essay might not even resemble what you were *told* was acceptable by your teachers or counselors.

Each of those other pieces of writing has its own set of rules: How many pages should it be? What should my introduction look like? How should each paragraph be structured? Where does my "thesis statement" go?

Your college essay, on the other hand, is more flexible, and is more of a story. It's very short, and you've got to make this one interesting. *So* interesting that when someone on an admissions committee reads it, he or she says, "Wow! That's a neat kid; I want that student to be a part of our school."

And before you can write that incredible essay, you need to have a topic.

While everyone has his or her own idea about the "ideal" college essay topic, there are certain basic elements that all admissions officers seem to find important. We've condensed these into three basic rules....

The Three Rules of Choosing a College Essay Topic

Rule #1: Your essay must be about *you*.

Sounds obvious, right? Are you going to write your essay about someone else? Of course not. But this first point is the most important one, and the one most often mishandled by smart kids (and good writers!) who manage to flub this great opportunity to sell themselves.

First-rate, successful college essays let their audience—the admissions officers we talked about earlier—learn a lot more about the candidate. Other than your essay, you're going to send these colleges your grades, your test scores, a couple of recommendations, a short list of your activities, and that's about it. How well do those things represent who you are? Do those five pages or so of information describe the real you?

When you write an essay that resonates at a human level—one that's from the heart and gives readers some insight into your personality—you give them a reason to like you, to understand you, and to want to admit you into their school. When you submit a well-written paper about something or someone other than yourself, you're only telling them that you're skilled at writing papers—information they can get elsewhere.

If you think this first rule is silly and easy and *of course you're going to write about yourself,* keep reading. Writing an essay that really gives insight into your personality is harder than you think.

What are some essay topics that obey Rule #1?

- **Claudia** wrote about how her experience working with disadvantaged children changed the way she views various aspects of her life.

- **Will** wrote about how tennis had dominated his life since childhood and what it took for him to quit playing when he had been so successful. Giving up his (and his parents') dream of playing professionally was the hardest decision he ever made.

- **Ashley** wrote about coping with a disability and how it affected her decision-making.

- **Ben** told a funny story that described how absent-minded he can be.

- **Fran** wrote a silly essay about how she hates the color pink.

After reading these essays, admissions officers undoubtedly felt as though they knew each of these applicants a little better. That's the key to *making the essay about you.*

It's not as though students who violate Rule #1 write about something entirely off-topic or impersonal. Rather, they write about some aspect of their lives, but in a way that doesn't really tell us much about them. We hear that they enjoy reading, or traveled throughout Europe, but we don't know how their attribute or experience makes them special. We're left thinking, "Anyone could have written that!"

Some examples of common essay topics that *don't work* because they're *too impersonal*:

- **Samantha** wrote about her grandmother and how—immigrating from Europe at age 14 and making a life for herself in Brooklyn—grandma has been a role model for Samantha as Samantha has grown up.

Samantha's essay is probably going to be a lot more about grandma than it is about Samantha. Even if we hear about their interactions, we're probably not going to learn much about what makes Samantha tick. Unless grandma's interested in starting college at age 85, this essay isn't going to help anyone.

- **Robert** wrote about biology, his favorite subject and likely major in college. He has a lot of biology-related predictions about what the future will hold.

Robert's essay is about biology. It *could* work if he opens up about himself, but unless Robert does something more unique than discuss current issues in the field, we're really not going to learn much about Robert here that couldn't be summed up in a few sentences. Robert, probably an interesting guy, may have wasted his essay.

- **Jessica** wrote about running on the track team and how wonderful it was when her school won the state championship; she loved being on a team and talked about how much better the experience was because it was shared among a group.

Jessica's essay is about teamwork and sharing joyous occasions. Most people probably share Jessica's opinion—while she might (but probably doesn't) have some philosophical insights, they're probably more about teamwork and running track than they are about Jessica. We're left knowing no more about this girl after reading the essay than before we picked it up.

So Rule #1 is easy enough: your essay must be *about you*. Remember—that doesn't just mean that you're the main character in the essay. Instead, you need to come across as a living, breathing human being—someone who can think about the past few years of his or her life and find something personal and revealing to write about.

The other components of your application let the admissions committees understand your background and—if you do a good job—be impressed by you. But the essays can help them *know* you and *identify* with you. This opportunity is too valuable to waste.

Rule #2: Your essay should be *interesting*.

When we ask students to brainstorm topics and they come back with something we tell them is "boring," we usually end up regretting having opened our mouths. Not only do we get hurt and disappointed looks from the student, but sometimes we get angry calls from mom or dad. Who are we to judge the value of their child's life? Who are we to say what's exciting and what isn't?

That's nonsense. We have yet to meet a high school student who didn't have anything interesting to say, but we've dealt with hundreds who have a hard time *articulating* what makes them special. And that's understandable. Thinking outside your daily life and routine is hard. Sometimes it's tough to imagine there's *anything* you could say that would interest the admissions committee of a prestigious college.

Of course, if you've done something truly unique in your life already, there's no reason to overcomplicate matters—you should probably write about that! If you competed in the Olympics, founded a charity, or started a significant business, you can bet the admissions committees will be eager to hear about such a formative experience. Writing the actual essay will still be challenging, but you've got your general subject matter already figured out.

Fortunately, for those among us with less newsworthy credentials, there's still hope. However, before we discuss which specific essay topics might work well, we're going to discuss which topics *not* too choose. Here, the most important thing to remember is to avoid the traps that make an essay unbearably *dull* or *common*.

Boring Essay Topics

- Don't write about the death of a pet, or even a family member. Not only are these subjects depressing, but such essays almost always sound the same.

- Don't think you need to necessarily write about the most important thing in your life. Many students tell us how important their friends, or siblings, are to them. Or they want to talk about their relationship with God. Even if you manage to make such an essay sufficiently personal to fit Rule #1, it's very challenging to write a "friends" or "God" essay that doesn't look like everyone else's. (Remember, these readers see *thousands* of essays in just a few months. Is yours special enough to leave an impression?)

- Beware the sports essay. We've seen good ones, but we've seen many more that put us to sleep before the end of the first paragraph. The thrill of victory. The agony of defeat. Persistence. Teamwork....It's all been done.

- The "I'm sitting down to write my essay, and don't know what to write about" essay. Yawn.

- Explaining that even though your parents are divorced, you now realize that they both still love you.

- Bad comedy. Your friends and family don't want to hurt your feelings, and so they often won't be the harsh critics you need. If most people reading it aren't laughing out loud, it's not funny.

In the end—and we'll talk more about this when we discuss particular topics—an interesting essay is simply one that stands out, engages the reader's attention, and leaves a lasting impression. It's not necessary to write about something super-impressive or particularly quirky. The key is to pursue some aspect of your life that sets you apart. And to provide as much detail and insight as you can.

Boring vs. Interesting Essay Topics

Boring	Interesting
During my two week trip to Europe, I learned a lot about various cultures.	During my two week trip to Europe, I learned a lot while trapped in a ski-lift for three hours with an elderly Iranian couple.
I learned the value of hard work by working summers in a warehouse.	I learned the value of hard work by working summers in a warehouse alongside three poor immigrants
I volunteer in a soup kitchen (too routine a topic unless you have something unexpected to say).	I started a soup kitchen because....
I'm a very well-rounded person—I'm not only good at academics, but I've also excelled at several sports and somehow find time to help the less fortunate. (not focused enough...doesn't get deep enough to be insightful)	To the outside world I appear to be a well-rounded person—but those very close to me know that I'm always just waiting for the opportunity to work on my mystery novel, which consumes all of my spare time.
I keep a fish tank, and it's a hobby I enjoy because I like animals and it looks nice. I've had the tank since my father bought it for me 10 years ago.	I have a fish tank with five fish named Lucky, Bob, Stripey, Homer, and Big Earl. Each of them has a personality, and in its own way reminds me of myself...
Growing up in a family of six children has taught me how to deal with others and the importance of family.	I live in a house with six children, but for the past four years, every Wednesday after soccer practice, I've eaten a special dinner alone with just my mom.

A note about passion...

What resonates when I read extraordinary essays from "ordinary" kids is that such essays often show *passion*. Passion is interesting, exciting, and real. Knowing what an applicant really cares about provides an insight that even the most detailed biography cannot. And a genuine passion for something usually demonstrates intellectual curiosity, a character trait prized by the admissions committees.

Does writing passionately about a subject mean that your essay will be interesting? Of course not. We've already mentioned how dull and routine the "my friends are the most important thing in my life" essay can be. And many high school students are passionate about music, yet admissions officers read 20 run-of-the-mill "I love music" essays for every good one.

The most important role of passion in your essays comes during the writing stage, when passion can infuse an already engaging essay with a rare urgency and humanity—we'll talk more about that later. But when you're still choosing a topic, it won't hurt to choose something you feel strongly about—a subject that you can discuss straight from the heart and with a special enthusiasm. That enthusiasm will come through when you write.

Rule #3: Your essay should say something not obvious from the rest of your application.

If you've paid close attention to the first two rules when selecting your topic, Rule #3 often isn't a problem. Yet, it's terribly important. The essay provides you with a great opportunity to talk about yourself in a format more personal and expressive than the rest of the application. If you waste that opportunity by rehashing your accomplishments, you're going to fall one step behind other applicants.

For students who have excelled primarily in one particular area, Rule #3 poses a dilemma. For example, an accomplished debater might really have something interesting to say about his debate experiences. On the other hand, this debater—by writing about debate—risks 1) wasting valuable essay space on something he's already conveyed elsewhere on his application and 2) foregoing the opportunity to talk about something else meaningful to him—such as a very unusual relationship—that really doesn't fit anywhere else.

The solution is to weigh carefully the risks and rewards of writing about a subject you've already covered. Any such essay should convey at least some new information or insight.

Essay topic that overlaps too much with the rest of the application	Why to avoid it
I worked hard at tennis, rising from JV to quarterfinalist in the state tournament. I'm proud of my hard work.	You can convey on your extracurricular activities list that you rose from JV to state quarterfinalist, and everyone will assume that it must have been hard and you must be proud.
I have had significant academic accomplishments, and have proven myself as a talented young scientist in Mrs. Johnson's biology class.	You've taken three biology classes and Mrs. Johnson is writing you a recommendation. We're already aware of your enthusiasm and talent.
Working for the student newspaper, I've gone beyond the norm in seeking out very challenging stories such as increased gang violence in our neighborhood.	This could be a good essay, but you'd probably get most of it across in an activity description and possibly a clipping of one of your articles. If you've got something else to write about, you should take the opportunity to convey that as well.
Volunteering is important to me. I want to make a difference in my world. For example, I've already volunteered in the following ways....	We can read about what you've done on your application. The importance of volunteering to you can maybe be explained better in narrative form, but is there really enough insight or new information here to warrant using up your essay?

Essay topic that overlaps with the application but is probably OK	Why it's OK
While a counselor at a camp for disabled children, I formed a very special relationship with one girl in particular.	You've probably already shown the committee that you worked at the camp, and so it would be nice to talk about something else. But the lessons you learned from an unusual friendship (as opposed to general observation) can't really be conveyed on a chart.
I used to be shy and reserved, but becoming active in theater has had a positive impact on my life that extends far beyond school.	We already know the extent of your participation and success in theater. But the rest of your application (except *possibly* a recommendation from your drama teacher) isn't capable of demonstrating the importance this activity has had for you.
A lifelong violinist and soccer player, last year I had to make a very difficult choice about which of these two activities I would pursue full-time, with the hopes of becoming a professional.	Wow! What a decision for an eleventh grader.... We can already tell that you did very well in two activities and eventually dropped one, but your description of this issue will go far, far beyond what's apparent from the rest of your application.

Always remember that the essay is a tremendous opportunity to *improve* your application. Choose a topic that will allow you to buttress and add to the rest of your story.

Getting More Specific: How to approach the essay questions, and how to find a topic

The hardest part of our job is telling students that their essays—which they've often spent a great deal of time conceiving, writing, and editing—need to be completely rewritten. Usually, this happens when we're handed an essay that has absolutely no hope of conforming to all of the three rules we discussed in the previous chapter. Why do students choose boring, impersonal, or non-illuminating essay topics? Often they do so because they arbitrarily settled on a topic and began writing, perhaps with the encouragement of a parent or well-meaning teacher. But on many occasions, we find that the student felt constrained by the essay question itself.

Each essay written for a college application does one of the following:

1. It responds to a particular question.

2. It responds to one of several particular questions.

3. It responds to a general request for an essay about almost any topic.

Recent Common Application Questions (used by many colleges, both as part of the Common Application and as questions on their own applications)

1. Evaluate a significant experience, achievement, risk you have taken, or ethical dilemma you have faced and its impact on you.

2. Discuss some issue of personal, local, national, or international concern and its importance to you.

3. Indicate a person who has had a significant influence on you, and describe that influence.

4. Describe a character in fiction, an historical figure, or a creative work (as in art, music, science, and so forth) that has had an influence on you, and explain that influence.

5. Topic of your choice.

While students dealing with the Common Application might initially think they are deciding between several questions, in reality that "Topic of your choice" option means that *any* topic is fair game. Yes, you can send an essay about *any subject* to a Common Application school.

Yet 95% of the students we work with who have *lousy* essay topics for a Common Application school invariably have chosen one of the first four questions. Answering one of these questions is fine, and those prompts can serve to get creative juices flowing, but *don't just pick one of these questions and try to answer it no matter what!*

Own your essay.

When we say that you need to *own your essay*, we mean that you must conform your best ideas to the questions you're given, and not let the questions themselves dictate what you write. If your two major essay ideas are 1) your relationship with your autistic brother and 2) your love of painting, don't choose Common Application Question #1 and then wrack your brain for an ethical dilemma you've faced, completely ignoring that great essay fodder you've already found.

Students who choose *questions* before *topics* sometimes write good essays, but they often don't do the best job of portraying themselves to the admissions committees. If chess is your best essay topic, then write about chess! Sometimes, this will be impossible, such as when you are asked to answer a question about, say, an issue of international importance (any way you slice it, chess is probably not an issue of international importance). But usually, you'll be able to find a way to write about one of your preferred topics.

This is *so* important that we can't stress it enough. *Owning your essay* is the key to putting your best foot forward. Don't waste your big essay opportunity discussing a book, historical figure, or social problem that means nothing to you.

The Specific Essay Questions

Of course, you may still face some limitations imposed by specific essay questions. So let's go through some popular questions to illustrate how they might be approached. We're not going to focus here on the Common Application questions, except to the extent they turn up elsewhere, because as we saw above *the Common Application places no limitations on the essay*. If you're simply dealing with the Common Application, you should write about your #1 topic, in whatever manner will serve you best.

Of your work, volunteer, and extracurricular activities, which has been the most meaningful, and why?

This is a very common question that appears in some form on a number of applications, usually as a shorter essay. And it's very straightforward.

Choosing a topic here is generally as simple as choosing your most impressive activity and one that credibly has had an intellectual impact on you. Spend most of your time with the debate team? Working at the hospital? Tutoring? As long as the three rules apply, it's all fair game.

One thing to consider when faced with this type of question is how it's likely to overlap with the other essays. On the 2004-2005 University of Michigan application, a similar prompt to the one above asked for a 250-word essay, while applicants were later asked to write a 500-word personal statement. If you had a very poignant experience working on the school play that fit well into the longer essay, you'd probably want to avoid the whole subject of theater here; as Rule #3 tells us, we don't want to waste time writing about a subject that's already well covered.

If you wrote a 300-page autobiography, what would be on page 137?

This question tries to stimulate a little creative thinking. It can also probably be answered in two ways: you can describe an important event in your life, or you can describe a hypothetical event that has yet to take place.

If you choose to write about the past, you want to make sure you follow Rule #2 and make it *interesting!* Give your audience some context, as well as some drama or suspense. If you're writing about your first day broadcasting on the student radio station, show how that day fit into your life and why it was an important moment. Dry autobiographies are painful to read.

If you write about the future, it's hard to avoid being at least a little interesting. Your bigger concern would instead be following Rule #1, and making sure that the essay is about your own life. Don't write about landing on Mars if you have no credible interest in space exploration. Don't write about being the first woman President if it doesn't follow from the rest of your application. A good autobiographical "page" about the future might describe a former biology student taking part in the cure of a genetic disease, or a former animal shelter volunteer running a charity for abused animals. Try to give some insight into your dreams and ambitions—the person you are today—through your description of the future.

Whatever route you choose, take advantage of the question format to be as creative as possible. You can refer to other unwritten parts of the "autobiography." You can begin or end mid-sentence. Here and on other unusual questions, you will be partially judged on the creativity and vigor with which you tackle the assignment. Put your imagination to work!

If you had to come up with a personal motto that defined a value you hold deeply, what would it be?

or

Choose a famous quotation that you find meaningful.

Some questions are designed to make you choose a value or belief that's important to you. In asking this type of question, the admissions committees are hoping to elicit from you—in a more philosophical way—what you find important.

There's room for a great deal of flexibility here. Good college essays often discuss learning and growth experiences, or defining moments or personal qualities. These fit well with the values/beliefs/quotations type of essay.

Here are some values applicants often write about:

- Commitment

- Charity/Helping Others
- Learning/Education
- Family/Friends/Love
- Compassion/Kindness
- Hard Work
- Happiness
- Perspective
- Loyalty
- Personal Growth
- Honesty/Integrity
- Humor

To find quotations, you can search the Internet (probably the best method) or else pick up a copy of *Bartlett's Familiar Quotations* and start leafing through the index.

The best way to succeed with this type of essay is to decide what you want to write, at least in very broad terms, and then work backwards to fit the topic. Starting with a value or quotation and then deciding how to write about it likely means you'll end up with an essay *that you don't own*. Remember—don't be controlled by the question prompt!

Bad answers to this question happen when an applicant's thought process goes something like this:

"What's a value I believe in? The importance of family. Why don't I write about how important my family is to me?" Or *"I always liked that Mark Twain quote...why don't I write about how that fits my life?"*

Being forced to answer a particular essay prompt does *not* absolve you of the responsibility to write a fantastic, A+ essay that will stand on its own. If you've brainstormed topics and your best stuff comes from your experience with music, then *write about that!* The quotation can be something about music or art. If you live and breathe fish, you should write about fish. Find an appropriate quotation. Can't find one? Keep looking!

Own your topic.

Discuss a setback or disappointment in your life.

This type of question shows up frequently on applications, often as one option among two or three. Generally, we advise applicants to avoid it unless they have something interesting and not too damaging to write about. "Ethical failures," such as the time you cheated on a test and got caught (and learned your lesson), do not make good essays; instead, they highlight what will probably be viewed as a flaw in your character. Setbacks that make you look impotent or incompetent, while not universally off-limits, more often hurt you more than they help: examples include your struggle to make a JV sports team, or your social or academic difficulties.

We *have* read some great essays that respond to this question, and what they all have in common is a real sense of personal growth and self-awareness.

- **Deb** wrote about her realization that she wasn't ever going to be a great golfer and how she quit the team. She had a number of other interests, and finally facing the disappointment of her father enabled her to focus on what was important to her as an individual.

- **Javier** wrote about being so nervous about public speaking that he was forced to cancel a speech he was to give at his confirmation ceremony. Angry with himself, he joined an adult speakers' club and took courses in speech and debate at his high school. For the past two years, he has given talks to freshmen and sophomores about overcoming his fear.

The best failure/setback essays put the negative event in the context of an eventual success or genuinely transformative learning experience.

Why is [insert college here] a good match for you?

One of the most straightforward of the essay questions, this is also one of the hardest to pull off well. This essay is usually shorter—often 250 words or fewer. The challenge is to avoid a generic answer and try to explain why a particular college is right for you (and by implication why other colleges aren't as good a fit). You should usually include more than one reason why Perfect University is the school of your dreams.

Here are some ideas:

- I need a big/small school because...
- I need a/an urban/rural/suburban school because...
- The [science/writing/history] program is appealing to me because...
- I visited and loved the...
- My family has long had connections to this school...
- I've talked to Coach Smith and am excited about playing on your basketball team.
- You have the best drama program in the area.
- You have the only marine biology program in the area.
- I want to work with professors Johnson and Chang in the biology department.

Bad Answers:

- Your school has great sports teams for which I've cheered since I was little.
- I want to live far from home and Florida is very far from Seattle.
- All of my friends are going to your school, too.

To some extent, our three rules of choosing a topic may be difficult to apply here. But remember that this essay should still mostly be about you. The colleges ask this question because they want to know that you've thought a lot about their institution and are eager to attend. The best answers explain the school's qualities in the context of the applicant's needs and ambitions. Saying you're excited about a biology program is only useful if you've already demonstrated an interest in biology. Otherwise, you haven't done anything to shine a light onto your own life and experiences.

Discuss an issue that is important to you.

This is a tough one, because it's difficult to integrate yourself and an "issue" into the same essay. So applicants sometimes just say: "Well, it asks for an important issue, so I'll talk about an important issue. I've always felt that AIDS in Africa was a problem because..."

Bad idea.

While you could write a solid and persuasive essay about a number of outstanding social or political concerns, you don't want to give away your essay-writing opportunity by ignoring Rule #3 and not teaching the admissions committees anything about you (the fact that you're against AIDS or hunger does not make you special).

You may recognize this question as similar to one on the Common Application. If you're seeing it there or as one of a number of choices on a school-specific application, and you don't know how you're going to approach it, you may want to consider one of your other options.

If you're stuck with this question, or feel that you have a good response, then you should tackle it with the same intellectual rigor that you would use for any other question. As always, your answer needs to be 1) about you, 2) interesting, and 3) not obvious from the rest of your application.

How can this be done? Here are a few essays that worked:

- **Sara** discussed heart disease. She has been active in charities related to heart disease since her father survived a heart attack. She's also done a great deal of research and has strong opinions related to funding and public awareness.

- **Greg** is an environmentalist with a lot of experience in that area.

- **Harold** wrote about his autistic brother, an area of personal concern for him.

- **Shelley** has never been involved officially in politics, but is constantly reading political journals and debates fiercely with all of her friends and family (she's the only Republican she knows).

The common thread here is a personal connection to the topic being discussed. By demonstrating passion for a particular issue, you show involvement in your world and that you care about events that take place beyond your own little bubble.

Put your best foot forward

Honesty is important, in college applications as much as anywhere. If you're dishonest on your applications, you'll not only face your own conscience, but you're also likely shooting yourself in the foot: one call to your high school from an admissions officer and suddenly *all* of your applications—and your academic future—will be in jeopardy.

However, many students are obsessed with portraying themselves as directly as possible to the admissions committees. They feel compelled to help the committees get to know "the real me." If they're asked what their most defining value is, they write about their most defining value. If the application wants to know which activity means the most to them, then that's what they put down on paper.

Of course committees want to know the real you! How else will they know whether you should be admitted or rejected? If you're going to be a superstar in college, they want to discover the real you so that they can quickly admit you into their class. But if you're a person with lesser credentials and promise, they want to know *that* too—so they can politely reject you and keep looking for someone better.

Unless you're perfect, your job is to portray an idealized version of yourself to the admissions committees. That doesn't mean you should iron out your faults and quirks to display a boring and flawless version of yourself. But it does mean that you need to exercise some control over how you are viewed during the application process.

Here are some tips for making the best possible impression:

- **Avoid displaying major character flaws or weaknesses unless it's necessary.** If you don't fit in socially or don't speak English well, try to avoid discussing it. If you're asked about your greatest weakness, don't say you're a compulsive liar—talk instead about something more benign, such as your trouble confronting people.

- **Sound like an interesting person, even on the short questions.** "Hanging out with my friends" is never a good answer for what you most like to do in your spare time, even if it's true.

- **When possible, choose your best activity instead of the one they ask about.** You may be asked to discuss the activity that is the most important to you. For the purposes of your application, starting a charity is more important than babysitting. Creative writing is more important than shopping. Don't avoid out-of-the-way interests that might make good essays, or feel compelled to write about your most "impressive" accomplishment. But remember to give your first priority to creating the best possible application, and not to deciding which of two activities is technically the most important.

- **Think creatively about your accomplishments.** Never lie about what you've done. But it's happened at least a hundred times: we'll be talking to a student in our offices and she'll list the things she's been involved with for the past few years. She'll mention JV volleyball, choir, church youth group, and then—in the middle of a list of about 20 minor activities—she'll throw out, "oh yeah, and in the summer before tenth grade my friends and I set up a Shakespeare class for inner-city kids, just once a week, as a project for our youth group." Because it only lasted for a few weeks, took little of her time, and happened over two years ago, she'll consider it almost not worth mentioning. But expressed properly to an admissions committee, this is gold.

- **Pick the question for which you can give the best answer, not the one you can answer the most easily.** Sometimes it's tempting to write about, say, the person who has most influenced you (simple—your older sister!), when the other questions—such as "Please respond to the following quotation from Emily Dickinson."—sound intimidating. But you need to resist the impulse to take the easy road. Spend some time and come up with your *best* answer, not the most obvious or "honest" one.

Putting together a great application is largely about writing essays that show committees what kind of person they'd be admitting to their school. When choosing a topic for *your* essays, focus on showing them an applicant they'd be proud to admit.

The Brainstorming Process

When we work with a student, we have a number of questions we use to try to draw out any experiences that might turn into good essay topics. How should you do this on your own?

The best way is to make a list. Take a sheet of paper and label it:

Essay Topic Brainstorming

On this paper you're going to put anything you can think of that might serve as material for one of your essays.

Then start putting the ideas down on paper. The first few should be easy—just answer the following questions. What are your activities? Your academic interests? Your jobs? What do you do in your spare time? How would you describe yourself? How would others describe you?

Write each topic along the left margin of your page, and leave yourself room to explore each idea. To the right of each idea (e.g. "Debate," "Dance," "Brother," "Chemistry," "Job at senior citizens' center," "Competitive," "Musical"), fill in details about where you think each subject could lead. Next to "Debate," for example, you might write the following:

- finally found an arena where I could express my opinions
- learned lessons of civility, respect for others
- first experience being on a real team
- learned the value of commitment and working hard on something

At this point, don't worry so much about the rules of essay writing or what might make a good topic. You'll be better off just scribbling down everything that occurs to you—good, bad, *or* ugly—and eliminating all the junk later. Sometimes an idea seems terrible at first and eventually leads to something creative or insightful.

Spend a few days on this. Think about ideas when you're taking a shower and when you're lying in bed at night. Each time you sit down to brainstorm, don't let yourself get up until you've had a few ideas.

Eventually, you'll hit a roadblock. Here are some idea starters to make sure you've covered all of your bases.

- **Academics.** What have you done in school that's truly influenced you? Are you a budding physicist? A reader? A writer? Have you won awards or accolades for any school work you've done? What are your academic interests?

- **Extracurricular.** What school-related activities have you involved yourself with? The big ones will be easy, but is there anything else you've either forgotten about or hadn't considered important? German Club? Math competitions? What sports have you played at any level?

- **Jobs.** What jobs have you had, both paid and unpaid? Include school-year positions as well as summer jobs. Don't forget about jobs you've had for only a short period of time (one week externships, small projects, and so forth)

- **Other Activities.** What do you do in your free time? Read? Program computers? Build models? Sew? Dance? Play sports that you don't play at school? Church activities? Take classes somewhere?

- **Who are the people who have had an impact on you?** Family members? Probably not friends unless there are some unusual circumstances. Have you had teachers who have been terrific mentors? How about employers? Role models? We've already discussed the dangers of discussing relationships in an essay, but it's worth writing everything down and seeing where it leads.

- **Travel.** Where have you gone? What did you do? Did you learn anything?

- **How would you describe yourself? How would others describe you?** Are there specific aspects of your life or personality that might be interesting to discuss?

- **What are some of your strongest memories?**

- **What do you like doing the most? Hate doing the most?**

- **What are your short-term and long-term goals?**

- **Who are your heroes?**

- **Are you artistic in any way? How so?**

- **What issues in the world are important to you?**

It's not important that you answer all of these questions, and you can certainly add to the list. The goal is to come up with a list of topics—as long as possible—that covers just about everything interesting or noteworthy that you could ever say about yourself.

Conclusion—settling on the right topic

So now you've got a list of topics. Some of them seem completely worthless ("I wrote that I love my grandma," you're thinking. "That is *not* a good essay topic!") Some look intriguing, but you're not sure how it might be turned into an essay. Hopefully, a few ideas appear promising.

Now's the time to bring it all together. Everything you've absorbed in this chapter can now be put to use, as you look at the questions you need to answer and try to adapt a topic from your list.

Good luck, and don't forget what we discussed in this chapter.

- **When choosing a topic, remember our three rules of choosing a good topic for your college essay:**
  1. The essay must be about you,
  2. The essay must be interesting, and
  3. The essay must be about something not obvious from your application.

- **Own your essay.** Pay attention to the questions, but write what *you* want to write.

- **Put your best foot forward.** Never lie or exaggerate the truth. But also never forget that you're trying to put together the best and most persuasive application, not the most technically "accurate."

- **Structure your brainstorming process.** Don't just read a question, think of an answer, and begin to write. To properly mine your entire life for good admissions essay fodder, you need to create a written list of all possible topics and give yourself some time.

Finding an topic is, in our opinion, the hardest part of the process. Once you've done that, you're ready to put together that perfect essay!

3

Writing: Putting your Thoughts on Paper

So you've got a topic. You've got a computer. You've got some time.

What now?

After settling on a topic, every applicant seems to have a different way to get started. Sometimes, students sit in front of a computer for hours, not knowing where to begin. Others work in fitful spurts, churning out an introduction or a conclusion but not much else. Sometimes we see outlines that undergo dozens of revisions. A few times a year, a student leaves our offices and returns the next day with a first draft. Some can't even get that first sentence written.

Unfortunately, there's no ideal approach. Writing the college essays is hard, and unless you've got everything planned out exactly in your mind, it's going to take some time to get that ideal 200-500 word essay on paper.

Following are some guidelines that our students have found effective over the years.

Give your essays the attention they deserve.

Writing is difficult. This is your first time writing a college admissions essay. The college admissions essay is likely the most important writing assignment you've ever had.

Your full attention is warranted.

Kids today have full schedules, and we know there are a lot of important things going on junior and senior year. But almost all of those sports, lessons, and activities should really take a backseat to turning out stellar applications. It's *that* important.

Don't wait until the last minute.

By far the most important timing issue related to your essays is *getting started early.* You can't wait until the last minute and still expect to turn out essays that will impress the admissions committees. Sure, you may be able to come up with something decent, just as you've probably written papers and studied for tests successfully by staying up very late. But this is a project for which you *must* get an A+. The college at which you may spend the next four years may very well be determined by how much time you leave yourself for the essays.

When should you begin? If your deadline is January 1, as it is for many competitive schools, you should start your brainstorming process no later than the middle of October. By the time November rolls around, you should have topic ideas for each essay and should be working to get each one started.

Why so early? Because writing these essays takes a long, long time:

- It takes a long time to find the right approach—sometimes *weeks* of writer's block.

- Writing the essay itself is time-intensive.

- You can easily spend weeks editing and soliciting feedback, and still not feel as though you've done enough.

- Sometimes, a seemingly good topic just doesn't lead to a great essay, and you need to start over.

- Other time-consuming issues, both admissions-related and not, always pop up.

Some schools, especially those with rolling admissions, insist that applications sent in earlier will get more attention. This alone is a good enough reason for you to get started as soon as you can.

Give yourself the space and time to work effectively.

The completion of any great project requires tremendous *focus* on the part of its creator. Sure, J.K. Rowling may have scribbled out the first *Harry Potter* books while sipping coffee in a London café. But she is a uniquely gifted author, and this was even for her probably quite hard to do—it's a safe bet that at this point in time, the *Harry Potter* sequels are written in a quiet office, without distractions, and with a certain amount of time each day set aside just for writing.

You need to create a schedule and a working environment where you can focus your attention fully on your essays. That doesn't mean you need to clear out a room in your house, or lock yourself in the basement for three hours each day. But when you sit down to write, you need to make certain you won't be distracted or interrupted. That means no TV, no video games, no phone calls, and (yes, we're getting ourselves in trouble here) no homework. Also, no working on grandma's kitchen table while everyone watches football during Thanksgiving weekend.

Some people will tell you to set aside a particular block of time each day (for example, two hours right after school). Unless you have serious self-discipline problems, that probably isn't necessary. But it's important to work in a quiet environment with plenty of room to spread out and where you won't be interrupted. When you sit down to write your essay, you should know that you won't need to do anything else for the next hour or two and can devote yourself fully to the task at hand.

Focus is essential.

Let ideas marinate.

The #1 excuse for bad essays? "I knew what I wanted to say, but I just couldn't put it down on paper."

One of the best things about starting early is that you can always take breaks when the creative process isn't going well. While you shouldn't use this as an excuse to procrastinate, the best strategy when you hit a major roadblock is to get up, relax, and try again later.

Sometimes ideas come to us in the car, or during a run. Often a student will try for weeks to write a first sentence, and then one day she'll sit down and write a beautiful essay in about three hours. These things take time, and your brain can't be prodded to do all of its preparation and creative work at once.

Along similar lines, you should avoid forcing yourself to get everything done in one sitting. You don't want to put yourself in this common predicament: "This Saturday I'm going to write a rough draft of my Notre Dame and Tufts essays, no matter what!" What if you're not writing well that day? What if one essay goes well but the other just doesn't seem like your best stuff? Sitting in your bedroom, staring at a blank sheet of paper, is not the way to encourage a stroke of creative genius.

Eventually, your mind will snap to attention and demand that you put pen to paper. Make sure that moment happens before, and not after, your final deadlines.

Write long.

When you look at word and page limits, always plan on your first draft being *longer* than it needs to be. Essays are almost always better for being shortened, and it's very satisfying to take out the worst parts of your essay and still be left with a piece that's the right length. If your first draft is the exact length you need, you'll be stuck with everything you wrote; if it's too short, you'll have to awkwardly fill it in somewhere.

Don't procrastinate.

This one is obvious. Just because you're not going to "force it" doesn't mean you can set up your work area, think about essays for a little while, and then go watch TV. If you avoid working on this difficult and time-intensive task, you'll end up in the same position as someone who waited until the last minute (and you'll be wishing in April that you could do it all over again).

Good Essay-Writing Habits

- Start early—at least two months before your essays are due.
- Sit down to work only when you'll have at least 60-90 minutes of completely uninterrupted time.
- Create a workspace that is non-distracting and free of clutter.
- If you're stuck, leave your writing for a while and return when you're more fresh.
- But don't procrastinate.

4

Format, Structure, and Style

Since you've never written a college admissions essay before, you probably aren't exactly sure what it's supposed to look like. Should it be a story? A paper? Do you need an intro? Should it be in the first person? Should you start with a quotation? Do you need a conclusion?

Believe it or not, there aren't a lot of great answers to these questions. Perhaps *because* no high school junior or senior has experience writing these essays, they tend to be much more diverse in style than, say, history papers or newspaper columns. And that's a good thing—no admissions officer wants to read a bunch of essays that all look the same.

Nevertheless, it helps to have *some* idea what's expected of you. We have included in the back of this book some "successful" essays that can give you a sense of what works. If you still want to see even more good essays, you can go online or purchase one of many books available that include sample college essays. Be careful, though—trying to apply someone else's creative format to your experiences is a recipe for disaster. And, potentially, an invitation to a charge of plagiarism.

Here are the basics for understanding how a college essay should—and shouldn't—be put together:

Structure

High school teachers will frequently suggest a fairly rigid format for any essay you write, which can usually be outlined something like this:

   I. Introduction

   II. Idea

      A. Sub-idea

      B. Sub-idea

   III. Another Idea

   IV. Yet another Idea

      A. Sub-idea

      B. Sub-idea

      C. Sub-idea

   V. Conclusion

Each idea is usually a paragraph—the outline above would thus be a five-paragraph essay. So if you're going to write an essay about your cat, your English teacher would probably want you to outline it like this.

   I. Introduction—I love my cat

   II. I've known her forever

      A. My parents brought her home when I was 4

      B. I can't remember life before we had her.

   III. She is cute.

   IV. She is smart

      A. She aced her cat IQ test

      B. She can juggle balls of yarn

      C. She always finds the catnip we hide

   V. For all of these reasons, I love my cat.

For most high school writing, and for the new SAT and ACT writing tests, this format isn't terrible. But while we can imagine some college admissions essays maybe being organized like this, you probably should avoid such rigidity in your essay.

If you turn to some of the essays in the back of this book, you'll see that the most heartfelt and interesting ones could never have been written from this type of strict outline. Good college essays *progress*, rather than *transition*. Like good short stories, they are primarily about one thing. Introducing that thing, subdividing it, and then summarizing it is usually not the way to go.

Instead of adopting an inflexible, pre-planned structure, you should focus on creating an essay that has a clear start-to-finish path. The best way to understand this is to look at some admissions essays that you liked, and think about how they were structured.

Your Introduction

Your essay should have an introduction. But that doesn't mean you need an introductory paragraph that summarizes what the essay will be about. The best college essay introductions usually pull the reader immediately into the narrative, setting the stage for what will follow. Think about the effectiveness of the following two introductions:

Disadvantaged students often struggle academically. Because role models are often not available for them, they need help after school if they are to succeed. Therefore, some friends and I decided that we would start a program where we help kids after school with their homework and other issues. While it was hard at first, we eventually learned several important lessons. I believe that I am a better person for having had the experience.

It was the only time I've ever cried in public, and I did my best to hold back the tears. But when I saw Jack onstage receiving his junior high school diploma, I broke down. Just two years ago, this had seemed impossible.

Both introductions are well-written, and would be perfectly appropriate to include as the opening to a college essay. But the second one, in addition to having more emotional impact, does a better job of pulling the reader into the essay and setting a positive forward trajectory.

When writing your introduction, don't try to summarize the essay, but instead focus on *setting the stage* for the essay. Your introduction should make the reader want to keep reading.

Your Conclusion

We think the toughest part of writing the college essay is the conclusion. Sometimes, a conclusion comes naturally. If you're telling a story, the conclusion is usually the place where you explain how the event or ordeal you describe has affected your life. If you're discussing an important decision, the conclusion would be the place to reflect upon the impact of that decision.

But some essays just don't seem to want to conclude well. For example, if you're writing a quirky essay, then almost any ending risks sounding corny. If you're writing a highly emotional essay, many endings may seem too formal or unsatisfying. What you want to do is wrap the essay up tightly in the same style as the rest of the essay, and "leave 'em laughing." Or crying. Or at least nodding.

It's the same problem that comedians face, as well as comedy sketch-writers and opinion columnists. You don't necessarily need a zinger, but you want a final thought that lets you leave on a high note. You probably know exactly what we're talking about: whether at a wedding, a funeral, or performance or in a magazine, we've all seen "good endings" that made us appreciate the skill of the writer. That's what you want.

And because coming up with that type of ending is much harder than it looks, writing a conclusion for certain types of college essays can be incredibly frustrating.

The best we can recommend is to *give it time*. Usually, a good conclusion will come to you if you take the pressure off of yourself for a few days. The most important thing is to recognize that your essay needs to conclude in a manner that's satisfying to the reader, and to avoid the temptation—whether in capitulation or deadline-induced panic—to conclude an otherwise superb essay with a trite and standard ending.

Some bad conclusions:

And because of all the lessons I learned from that experience, I feel that I am now ready for college.

And that's the story of why I quit the volleyball team.

Well, it's time to get back to my busy life. Hope to see you soon!

While I miss my grandfather very much, I know that a little part of him is with me wherever I go.

Conclusions, or at least concluding sentences, are more about style than substance. This is no place to try to interject a funny joke or complex, meaningful life lesson. Write something that wraps up your essay neatly, and leaves the reader satisfied that he or she just read something good.

For some examples of how a well-written admissions essay might conclude, take a look at the essays we included at the back of this book.

Poor structure means boring essays.

We already discussed how your essay topic should be interesting. Similarly, the structure you choose should *allow* it to be interesting. That doesn't mean using some crazy format or trying to make your essay different from every other one you've read. But it *does* mean that you should make sure your essay flows forward and stays alive for the reader.

The most boring essays are either overly structured (such as any essay you feel you could predict after reading the first paragraph), or very unstructured (think: meandering essay about all the reasons someone likes basketball). The most interesting essays progress from an introduction, through a logical and sequential thought process, into an orderly conclusion. They're paced well. Their structure gives them a life of their own. The advice we most frequently give our clients on the subject of structure is this: "tell a story."

Style

We've seen excellent college essays written in just about every tone, style, and type you could imagine. Funny. Sad. Dead serious. Slice-of-life. Narrative. Sarcastic. Literary. Intentionally simple. Long. Short. Formal. Casual. Very casual. With dialogue. With transcribed sound effects. With many characters. With many animal characters. In the first person. In the third person. In the second person. Angry. Ecstatic. Plain. Cryptic. Symbolic. Ambiguous.

There are few concrete rules for writing the college essay: as long as your product demonstrates that you are a good writer and would be a good fit at the school to which you're applying, almost any approach is fair game. Yet while every tactic and every essay-writing strategy could probably be applied successfully to a given essay, there are some basic rules about how you should write.

Writing a "clever" or "funny" essay raises the bar considerably

In principle, there's nothing wrong with writing a funny college essay, or one that takes an interesting and unusual approach. The problem is that few students are successful in constructing such essays, and they thus rarely have the intended impact upon the admissions committees.

First of all, pieces written in a "funny" style usually simply don't work from a comedy perspective. They're not funny. That's because 1) even funny students usually aren't experienced at writing comedy bits, 2) senses of humor vary widely, especially between different generations, and, sadly, but true, 3) most people aren't funny.

Unfunny comedy essays, or other unsuccessful attempts at being clever or original, demonstrate a lack of self-awareness or knowledge about the admissions process. It's one thing to be unfunny; it's a whole different thing to be unfunny but to think that you're funny. You don't want the admissions officers' first impression of you to be that you're a poor comedian who thinks he or she has material so great that it's worthy of a college application.

Second, writing something clever or funny distracts you from other tasks you could be pursuing in an essay, such as explaining something you've accomplished, revealing something substantive about your personality, or telling a story that demonstrates something about your experiences. You wouldn't submit a hilarious two-page joke for your essay, even though it was hilarious; similarly, you shouldn't submit a funny essay that doesn't accomplish anything other than amuse the reader.

The best way to inject comedy, quirkiness, or originality into your essay is to do so *subtly*, in the context of your broader effort to put together a good essay. Let them know that you're clever or funny if you feel that's important, but don't make it your defining characteristic. That means that there's less pressure for you to succeed on that front, and more opportunity for you to demonstrate your overall personality, skills, and value as a candidate.

Casual vs. formal style?

This is a common question. Obviously, writing in a more casual style allows the writer to connect better with his or her audience. On the other hand, some students become concerned that writing too informally will turn off admissions committees: these students have been trained to write in a relatively formalistic way, and can't imagine doing otherwise on such an important assignment.

Not surprisingly, the answer is that you need to achieve a happy medium. Writing too formally constricts your essay and makes it difficult to establish a relationship with your reader. Writing too *in*formally, however, can indicate a lack of respect for the process and signal to the admissions committees that you lack the savvy or ability to properly use the English language.

Here are some frequently asked questions about formal versus informal writing on essays, and our answers:

Can I write my essay in the first person (e.g. use the word "I")?

Absolutely. The first person creates a more intimate tone and is generally used in admissions essays.

Should I refer to the admissions committees in my essays (for example, "If you accept me to your school…")

Probably not. While it's important to understand who your audience is, addressing them directly breaks the mood of what should be an important and thoughtful piece of writing. It's also very unusual, at least in good essays.

Can/should I start my essay with a famous quotation?

Unless you've been specifically asked to do so, we generally recommend avoiding quotations. Starting with a quotation from *Bartlett's* is very common in mediocre essays and will look *very* familiar to weary admissions officers hoping for something original. If you use a quotation, it should be done very well and should be germane to your essay.

Especially avoid claiming that you've lived your life by a particular quotation or mantra, even if it's true. It's just too trite.

Is slang/vernacular okay?

Sometimes, but usually not. If you're writing dialogue for some reason, or trying to convey the way a particular person talked, it might be okay. But don't use phrases such as "I was cool with that" or "He dissed my friends." Not only does casual slang indicate that you may not have perfect command of the English language, but it also makes it look as though you're not savvy enough to write "up" to the admissions committees.

Anything else I should avoid?

Clichés ("I knew the early bird gets the worm"; "Practice makes perfect.")

Sarcasm, which usually doesn't come across well on paper.

Vulgarity

Length

You should always follow directions from the applications regarding the length of an essay. However, that usually doesn't mean you need to exactly hit word or page limits. If an essay asks for a certain number of pages, using your word processor you should be able to edit spacing, margins, and so forth to make the essay look good and properly fit into the right number of pages. But don't do anything that makes it appear that you were playing with those factors intentionally. Generally, you should have somewhere between 250 and 450 words on each page.

If you're asked to limit your essay to "around" a particular number of words, you should try to roughly hit that figure (unless the application is strict about the word limit). Our general rule is that your essay should be between 85% and 105% of the total word limit. That means that a 500-word essay should be between 425 and 525 words.

Technically, you can always make your essay shorter than the recommended length. But we don't recommend coming in much below ordinary word or page limits. Try to go *over* the recommend length, and then shorten your essay so that you're giving them roughly the maximum length they requested.

5

Writing Well

While everyone in the running at the most competitive colleges writes well, good writing remains the #1 factor in evaluating college essays, and is without a doubt the hallmark of any good college essay. Good writers demonstrate intelligence, thoughtfulness, and a finely-honed command of the English language. *Great* writers show, by writing with a skill and flair similar to that shown by past acceptees, that they belong at a prestigious school and have the skills to perform at the level that will be expected of them.

Bad essay writers, on the other hand, demonstrate that they did not care enough about their essays to make sure they were correctly written. It's tough to turn a good essay into a great one, but to make bad writing into decent writing is simply a matter of attention and focus. And if necessary, seeking help.

This short chapter will not attempt to teach you grammar, punctuation, or proper MLA style. Our thinking is that whatever you know about writing now is what you're probably going to take into the essay-writing process.

But even if you've paid attention to nothing we've written thus far, we want you to take heed of the following advice:

Your college essay should be the best piece of writing that you've ever produced. There should be no mistakes. There should be no awkward phrasing. Everything about the way your essay is written should indicate that you are an intelligent young person with a strong command of the language and an ability to put ideas to paper.

The following are our simple writing tips that you should keep in mind when putting together your essay.

Grammar/mechanics/usage

Your writing must be flawless. No improperly used semicolons. No incorrectly-used words. No problems with subject-verb agreement. Your pronouns must have antecedents. Your syntax must be clear. If you have questions about an issue, check with someone *who knows*. If you struggle even a little bit with these technical aspects of your writing, seek help after you write your first draft.

Vocabulary

Speaking like an intelligent young adult is important. But using big words that you don't ordinarily use is likely to get you in trouble. Admissions officers can spot instantly the student who is using big words when smaller ones would do just as well.

Admissions officers have told us that they've seen words such as "myriad," "comprise," and "nuance" (often used incorrectly) more than they care to remember. Speak plainly and in the language that enables you to most effectively convey your point.

For a great essay about clear and simple writing, read George Orwell's *Politics and the English Language*. Another great resource is Strunk & White's *Elements of Style*.

Active voice

Compare the following two sentences:

Vanilla was the flavor that I chose.

versus

I chose vanilla.

The first sentence is written in the *passive voice*, while the second is written in the *active voice*. For the purposes of your essay, you should always choose the active voice. Doing so makes your essay livelier, more fun to read, more interesting, and more indicative that you are an experienced writer.

Vary sentence length

An essay with only long and complex sentences is difficult to read. One with only short sentences sounds boring. The most interesting way to write is to have long sentences interspersed with short ones.

Gender-neutral language

Some people will be offended if you use masculine pronouns to represent an unknown person. On the other hand, using combined terms such as "him/her" can be awkward. Avoid both problems by rearranging your sentences to eliminate awkward or offensive constructions.

For example:

I was worried that after I met the admissions officer, he or she would decide I wasn't good enough for his or her school.

becomes

I was worried that the admissions officer would think I wasn't good enough for Stanford.

No mistakes

Your essay cannot contain a single spelling error, misused homonym (their/there), or improperly capitalized (or not capitalized) word. Don't assume that your spelling/grammar program on your word processor caught every mistake. Computers are notorious for allowing major errors to slip by for arcane reasons.

If you're not a great writer, it's going to be tough to write a great essay with absolutely no help, no matter how much time you put into it. Don't be afraid to seek assistance. Everyone loves to help a college applicant, and odds are good you know a teacher or family member who can help you improve the strength of your writing.

6

Review and Editing

"The first draft of anything is s**t."

—Ernest Hemingway

We just finished explaining that opening quotations and vulgarity should be avoided. So the fact that we start this short chapter by blatantly violating both rules should get your attention.

Of course Hemingway is exaggerating a little, or at least just expressing his opinion of his *own* writing. But it's definitely true that for most writers of any caliber, the first draft of an essay will be substantially worse than the carefully-improved final product.

For some applicants, guiding the admissions essay from the first draft through the version that eventually gets mailed to colleges is actually the hardest part of the process. That's because given the importance of this task, you're probably going to want to spend more time reviewing and polishing this essay than you have for anything else you've ever written.

Here are the steps:

Decide if what you've written is any good.

Most essays can be much improved through editing. But if what you've originally come up with seems terrible to you, it probably is; while lots of work might improve it, you'd probably be better off starting from scratch.

What makes an essay worth abandoning? Not mistakes—mistakes can be corrected. We generally recommend stopping work on an essay only when the essay has a fundamental problem that can't be corrected with partial or stylistic changes.

For example, if an essay is *very dull*, there's usually not much that can be done to make it interesting. The problem is unlikely to be related to how the essay was put together—rather, the choice of topic was probably ill-advised.

Your topic must be interesting. Sometimes you can't tell until you've written your essay that it just isn't going to work. In that case, despite all of your hard work to date, you need to scrap it and start over.

When else should you pull the plug? In addition to dull essays, the other type of essays that generally can't be improved are *impersonal* essays. If you realize after writing it that your essay doesn't really say anything about you or what type of person you are, you'll probably need to select a new topic and start over.

Put it in a drawer

When you've finally written your essay and have decided you've got what looks like a reasonable first draft, you should put the essay away for at least a few days—and preferably at least a week—and completely forget about it.

Looking at your essay again only when you're "fresh" will allow you to see it from the perspective of a reader, rather than someone who's been focused entirely upon being a writer. You'll have a better understanding of which sections are the most (and least) effective, and what sounds trite or forced. You'll also be more easily able to spot grammar and usage errors.

Edit

There are two stages to any good editing process:

A) Content editing

Editing an essay is more art than science: your task is simply to make the essay better, any way you can. At the content editing phase, that primarily means cutting, expanding, rearranging, and clarifying the various components of your essay to ensure that your essay is as interesting and readable as you can make it.

Read your essay over carefully and decide which parts you like best, and which parts seem not to work. Does it flow well? Is it focused, or do some sections seem not to fit with the rest? Have you spent enough time explaining all of the important points? Are there sections that—while well-written—don't really seem necessary?

The most important and underappreciated quality that all good college essays share is *focus*. *Focus* means that your essay is about one thing—it flows from one point to the next, not by meandering, but rather by building on what's come before.

The content editing stage is the perfect time to think seriously about focusing your essay. What's your point? If you could add one paragraph somewhere to make the whole essay flow better and make more sense, what would it be and where would it go? Are there parts that just don't click yet? Is every part of your essay *getting you something*, or are there parts that you'd be better of abandoning?

B) Line-by-line editing (or "stylistic" editing)

At this point, it's finally time to begin looking at the details of your essay. However much time you spent making sure that you were crafting each sentence as carefully as possible, there is always *a lot* you can do to make your essay read more elegantly.

This does *not* mean, as some students seem to think, unnecessarily complicating your vocabulary. It *does* mean making sure that each word is accurate and is there for a reason. Eliminate all spelling and grammar mistakes. Improve your transitions. Vary the sentence length. Essentially, implement all of the writing tips we talked about in the previous section.

Most good writers find that such editing is more easily done on a piece of paper than on a computer—editing on the computer, where each letter is changed immediately, can make it difficult to carefully consider the impact of each change. Print your essay, grab a pen, and pretend you're a tough writing instructor attempting to pick your own essay apart.

But don't forget that editing an essay is about more than eliminating mistakes. You don't want to reach for fancy sentence constructions and five syllable words, but you *do* want to add to and improve your writing—even if it's already pretty good. Make those sentences active. Think about what will create a more interesting essay. Ensure that you're not using the same sentence structure throughout each paragraph (for example, don't start every sentence with "I"). Make the introduction gripping. The conclusion satisfying. Ask yourself, "Is this something that a great writer would write?"

Seek Help

Should you ask other people to help you review your essay?

In a word, yes. Fresh (and often more experienced) eyes can be invaluable in providing constructive ideas, identifying weaknesses, and correcting mistakes that you've missed simply because you've grown too familiar with your essay.

But whom should you show it to, and what are you looking for from that person?

Show your essay to someone who 1) will be honest and 2) will know what he or she is talking about. The best choice would be someone involved in college admissions. That's usually impossible, so the next best choice is either an English teacher or a *very* smart friend who will have the energy and commitment to really review what you've put together. If that's not possible, show it to an adult who's willing to devote some time to you and will be honest.

If you can afford it and think it would help, hire an *ethical* professional admissions counselor (one who doesn't offer to write or rewrite your essay). We do this for a living, and don't charge nearly as much as some other folks. You can get started on our web site at www.brody.com.

Whomever you choose to read your essay, you'll need to tell your reader to be brutal. You're hoping that the reader can tell you:

1) which parts are the best
2) which parts are the worst
3) what's confusing
4) what's missing
5) what doesn't belong
6) where you've made errors

A general report on your essay ("I liked it!" or "You'll definitely get into Notre Dame" or "That story about deep-sea fishing was *so* interesting—I never knew that about you!") is, while often reassuring and nice to have, essentially worthless for the purpose of improving your essay.

What you want is detailed criticism and red ink. The more analysis and criticism you can get, the more opportunities you'll have to improve your essay.

Remember, though, that in the end *you* are responsible for the final product. Don't accept every suggestion given to you—instead think critically about your essay and decide which changes will actually make your essay better. Even adults make mistakes—and where writing is concerned, they make lots of them. You also don't want to make changes that, while technically correct, will destroy the flow, consistency, or readability of your essay.

That's it. Once you've given your own feedback and solicited that of others, and made every improvement you can envision, you're ready to send it out.

Good luck!

7

Successful Essays

Here we've compiled a number of college admissions essays we received from college students and clients. What do the essays have in common? Most notably, they're good. Without exception, the students writing these essays got into top colleges, and their essays probably helped. Don't let that intimidate you, though—everyone, regardless of what they've accomplished or their writing ability, can benefit from what these essays have to teach.

Why are we including them? We hope that by seeing how these students approached the task, and the diversity of their topics and styles, you'll understand better what the college essay is all about. After each essay, we discuss it briefly—why we liked it, what it's best qualities are, and what you as a future essay writer can take away from it.

Most of these essays contain minor errors that we, as full-time admissions counselors, would probably correct. However, because such issues are inevitable among even the best and brightest high school students, we generally focus here on what's important for you to learn. Think about what you, as a writer, might be able to absorb from these fine examples.

And enjoy.

Essay #1

A Dissection

I think that the first time that science really made sense was in seventh grade, when a frog lay splayed out on the desk in front of me. The stench of formaldehyde made my eyes water and my stomach churn, but I did not really notice, fascinated by the still form, its innards arranged in neat array under the flap I had incised in its abdomen. Inside were the precise engineering marvels, finer than the gearings within a Swiss watch, each perfectly evolved through a process I had only read about and never truly understood. Here was the basis for religion, the faith in a higher power that actually represents faith in the innumerable and incomprehensible wonders of nature.

I have always enjoyed observing patterns: the point and counterpoint in Beethoven's 15th string quartet and the intricate fingerings and crescendo in his Kreutzer sonata, for example, as well as the rise and fall of the empires of history. It is the intricate patterns of life, however, that particularly fascinate me, and my brief surgery on the frog led me to envision a career in medicine. On the surface it seems simple, painless (for the doctor), and rewarding; just put the jigsaw puzzle of life back together in some semblance of order: a drug here, an incision there, and the patient will be cured.

However, the flip side of the coin terrifies me: what if those jigsaw pieces will not fit back into place? What if something goes wrong, an artery bursts, the patient hemorrhages and dies within seconds? Science is beautiful in an abstract sense when dealing with grand theories, words on a page, even the peaceful revelations of the frog, but perhaps the frog was not a good analogy for the experience of medicine. After all, there was no danger; it had already passed on. If I had to explain to a grieving family why they have lost their young daughter, however, the crushing realities might become just a little too real.

Nevertheless, working hands-on would be more satisfying to me than to remain in abstraction, in a world that, while appealing in its lack of emotional trauma, offers relatively little in the way of direct human application and personal reward. Surely in medicine there must exist great triumphs, something to balance the overwhelming defeats. The common medical adage is that "it never gets easy." I suppose this is true. In a way, I hope that it is because, while some might believe that emotions cloud the mind of a superior doctor, I believe that to truly be a good doctor one must live in constant awe and fear. Those are emotions I possess in abundance: awe at the beauty of life and fear at its fragility.

This is an excellent college essay that helped its author get admitted to Harvard.

The first thing we noticed about this essay is that it's written incredibly well, demonstrating the author's impressive command of the English language—especially for a high school senior. "The stench of the formaldehyde" is palpable, and the reader is struck by the author's fascination by the frog's anatomy.

After hearing about this awakening experience, we're given a glimpse into how this intelligent young man thinks about his world. He listens to symphonies. He studies history. Better yet, while he's doing those things, he's observing and learning.

The author also has a precocious and well-developed sense of what he enjoys and what kind of person he is. He's a doctor-in-training, for one thing, who is fascinated by the "beauty" and "fragility" of life. Admissions officers don't expect high school students to have their careers planned at age 17, but if you're truly passionate for a field, that can provide insight into your personality and character. For this author, we have a real image of someone who knows what's important to him and where he wants to focus—academically, intellectually, and professionally.

Finally, it should be pointed out that, while there's definitely no specific formula for writing an excellent college essay, as admissions professionals we can say that this guy just feels like a Ivy League admit. The easy turns of phrase, vocabulary, diction, thematic cohesiveness, and effortless intellectual perspective are all marks of someone ready for a nationally elite college.

Lessons to take away from this essay:

1. Your essay doesn't have to be a story or about a specific incident or accomplishment.

This essay talks briefly about an experience from the seventh grade, but then is primarily about ideas and the passions of the author. We warn against generic essays because they don't always come across as plausible—describing your love of theater doesn't mean much if you don't have any experiences in theater and can't convince the reader that your "passion" isn't just a ploy to sound interesting to colleges. But this author's interest in biology and the delicate nature of life is almost tangible. It seems impossible that he's not being genuine, and it's likely that his extracurricular activities and academic record buttress this heartfelt essay. He also manages to link his abstract thoughts to tangible images ("a grieving family" and "an artery bursts," for example)—bringing the reader into his world and showing off unusual rhetorical skill.

2. Sounding smart matters.

Seeking vocabulary "home runs" is a common way to ruin your essay. Admissions officers can see right through attempts to sound smart and intellectual, and there's nothing worse than appearing phony or otherwise not genuine on your applications. When you use vocabulary words that are technically correct but could easily be replaced by simpler and shorter words, it demonstrates that you're writing in a certain way just to try to impress your reader.

However, as the saying goes, "If you've got it, flaunt it." The above essay is written so well that the author's command of the English language will be noted and will work in his favor. The sentences are well-constructed and vary in length and style. The writing is emotional and evocative without being awkward or difficult to understand. He has an impressive vocabulary and wields it like a well-practiced sword—not like the blunt instrument used by some high school students as they flip through their dictionaries. Here is someone who *must*, simply by virtue of the way he expresses his thoughts on paper, be intelligent, thoughtful, interesting, and intellectually capable.

Essay #2

My mother grew up on a farm, the daughter of a German-Swiss father and American-Swiss mother. My father immigrated to the United States from Cuba following the Communist revolution. Like all who grow up on farms, my mother has come to the belief that a teenage boy can do nothing better during the summer than toil away on a farm.

As such, the summer after my freshman year and each summer since, I have worked at Terry's Berries, a local organic farm.

It started out as a part-time job. I would work from eight in the morning until noon, then go home for lunch. Terry soon asked me to work a bit later and a bit later. Soon, seven became a better hour than eight. By the end of my first summer, I was working seven to four, Monday through Friday. Work I did.

The conversations with the other workers are among the greatest pleasures I have had. Each year, a new group of men would arrive, mostly Guatemalan or Mexican. I value what I have learned from them. Julio, for instance, showed me how to weed without ruining my back, and Manuel explained why I should always vote for Democrats.

Every summer, inevitably, I would be asked about my future. What did I plan to do? I always dreaded this question because I would hate to isolate myself by mentioning college or some profession I wished to pursue. "No sé." I don't know, I would answer. "Ve a la universidad," José would say. "Este es el alternativo." This is the alternative to the university, he said, gesturing to the fields.

It is not that there is no virtue in farming. Holly, another worker on the farm and a college graduate, views her work as fulfilling, and therefore has chosen farming as her way of life. But she made the choice to farm. José and his compatriots have been limited by circumstance, and so appreciate the choices afforded by education.

I hope José's words will always stick with me. They are a moving testament to the power of academic excellence. Beyond those professional inspirational speakers, the chats with my counselor and my parents' advice, José's simplicity has had the most profound effect on me. College gives me a choice in life, and a college of Harvard's magnitude gives me the most choices. Harvard fulfills my highest expectations of higher education, and I believe that my attendance there will satisfy José's mandate.

This author was also admitted to Harvard, but with a much different approach to the essay. While the first essay is intellectual and introspective, this applicant—the son of a Cuban immigrant—writes a much simpler story about working on a farm and what he learned during his time there.

The impressive aspect of this essay is that the applicant took a tough summer job that some would find tedious and apparently turned it into a tremendous learning experience. He understands how important his opportunities have been, and is grateful for the wisdom imparted to him by those less fortunate.

Lessons to take away from this essay:

1. It's possible to write about experiences with those less fortunate than you without sounding self-important or condescending.

The author of this essay comes across as relatively humble, and seems to have truly appreciated the lessons he learned from his co-workers such as Jose and Manuel. However, far more common are essays that reveal the author to be condescending or overly proud of his or her relatively small contribution to the plight of the homeless, disabled, or otherwise less fortunate.

Especially for those who have led a privileged childhood and adolescence, it's sometimes hard to recognize how skeptical others might be of your reflections on society (and rightfully so—it's not until you head out into the world that you'll really know what it's all about). Write about what you learned, and what it meant to you, and how it felt to be a part of a positive experience. But don't let admissions committee members think that you just put in a few hours of community service to bolster your resume, and that you naively think the world is noticeably better for it.

2. Those with "cultural diversity" should consider exploiting that advantage on their applications.

This lesson doesn't apply to everyone. But if it's relevant to you, you'll want to pay attention.

Colleges want to admit students with different life experiences. One of the most common and identifiable ways for a high school senior to have such experiences is to have a particular cultural or ethnic background.

When you tell a story about immigrating to America, or growing up among immigrants, it adds an extra dimension to your application. Not only do admissions officers often assume that you overcame some difficulties (such as poverty, language issues, or a tricky home situation) in getting to where you are today, but they'll also assume that you'll have something to teach your classmates about your culture, heritage, different worldview, or immigrant experience. This puts you at a unique advantage in comparison with other applicants.

3. You don't need to write about earth-shattering accomplishments.

While we encourage you to write about something impressive, it's not necessary for you to have performed surgery, rescued a drowning man, or won a national tennis tournament. "Regular" people get admitted into all types of schools (even Harvard), and these people simply write about experiences that provide a window into who they are.

The above essay is about nothing more significant than a low-paying summer job. But the author demonstrates not only that he was able to get something valuable from his experience, but also that he is someone who learns from his world, is appreciative of what he has been given, and will likely make good use of educational opportunities.

This applicant could have easily complained that he had "nothing to write about." Instead, he took an opportunity that would sound mundane to some, and wrote about it in an interesting and affecting way.

Essay #3

Analog

Although my relationship with video started before I was in high school, my tools have remained the same: beige Mac G3, video 8 camera, VCR, and AV cables. Most people making video today are using digital equipment. I'm still in analog. Quality is lost, and the picture that is finally imported looks like it was shot in the '70s.

Analog is all give and take. If the computer does not want to render full screen video, I just reduce the picture by half. If the computer will only play a few frames before it cuts out, I'll go take a walk. Working this way may be frustrating, but when the video performs, diced into tiny fast-moving segments, and the music gets poured over the top as if it is directing it, that's when I'm satisfied.

Analog is grainy, gritty, and shiny. Analog is beautiful the same way some graffiti art is, because it's real. These are all the things I love about it. And these are the reasons why analog is the place to which I return year after year.

I am not proud of my first efforts in film. The camera was my toy—a diversion to pass time, to occupy myself in a creative way. But these early films gave me experience. I gradually gained both the patience and maturity to create something I'd want to show to people other than my snickering friends.

My first real attempt, Gone Wrong, was a clumsy, hardly-edited, three-scene piece about a kid who gets hit in the "fundamentals." The soundtrack starts with an upbeat jam by Chick Corea but then shifts to a melancholy Gershwin song for the agony scene. Although the music was appropriate, it was not synched to details. The whole piece was unfocused and immature. I had gone out to have fun, not to create a work of art.

Though Gone Wrong was childish, it was my initiation into the feeling, rhythm, and method of editing. It was my first taste, my first negotiation, my first exchange. It was also my last film that would have dialog and an artificially-created story. Through my next two attempts, I realized I was much better at recording real life than creating one of my own.

When I look back on the days of Gone Wrong, I see myself as a child trying language for the first time. I made mistakes, but I was learning.

About a year later, I spent a Sunday taping my mom endlessly watering the garden, and my brother and dad intently building a soapbox car. I put the scene of my mom, and the scene of my brother and dad, into separate boxes on the same screen. The constant jumps between the two jaggedly-cut shots were a great way to show my family's compulsiveness. Each lasted only a few seconds before shifting angles. I chose Miles Davis' "Springville" as a soundtrack. It is a fanciful, carefree piece with a melancholic undertone. Then I edited all the quick cuts to match the music. The movie ended on the last note of the song.

Sunday *helped to establish my style. When I finished with it, I had an excellent technical and creative grasp of my workspace. However, as much as* Sunday *was a huge step forward from* Gone Wrong, *it was still immature. The quick cuts made the film almost overedited. It was as if, in my quest to show my family's obsessiveness, I had emulated them, becoming obsessive myself in the intricate construction of the film.*

I entered Sunday *in a student festival. I was surprised when it won first place in the nonfiction category. I think it won because, unlike many of the entries, it wasn't blatant.* Sunday *was about a family doing what families do. It was fanciful, escapist, and soothing. I could make subtle reference to conflict, without beating the ideas to death.*

The award gave me confidence to return once again to my place. By now, my old beige G3 and video 8 camera had become dated. Almost every entry in the South Bay Student Video Festival that year was made in digital video. People were telling me to upgrade, but I held out. My workspace and my equipment were my close companions. Migrating to digital would be a betrayal. I liked being an iconoclast, a stalwart for an obsolete medium. Plus, I loved that grainy quality of the videos. By going to the festival, and comparing my work to what else was out there, I realized that technology wasn't the only thing that set me apart. Not only were the technology and the methodology iconoclastic, so was I.

Sophomore year, I went on a trip to Las Vegas. There, I saw people mindlessly attached to slot machines. They weren't just playing, they had become robo-comatose regressed baby life forms captivated by the glowing lights and hypnotizing sounds. This gave me an idea for my next film. Unlike Sunday, *however, I had a plan for this movie.*

This idea slowly became Slot. *When I got back home, I once again approached my workspace. After* Sunday, *I knew how to work. I selected clips of the people who looked the most robotic, and started going through my CDs for music. By now, I had learned that, for me, editing, feeling, and mood for a film is patterned by, and expressed through the music. Even the length of the movie itself it defined by the length of the song. I decided to set* Slot *to Django Reinhardt's "Blues Clair," an upbeat jazz guitar composition that gave the film an ironic, turn-of-the-century feeling that complemented my trademark herky-jerky analog style—itself the byproduct of using old equipment. "Blues Clair" was perfect. In addition to its repetitive style, which aurally resembles slot machines, its structure virtually determined the outcome. For example, I set one of Reinhardt's guitar arpeggios to a video segment of a lounge pianist playing an arpeggio.* Slot *was smooth, gliding along to the swaying tempo.*

According to Kohlberg's Theory of Moral Development, the world becomes less about you as you grow up. Gone Wrong *was all about me. It was an infantile view of existence.* Sunday *was an insular look at family relationships, but still mostly about me.* Slot, *however, took a stance about the world and how we, as human beings, inhabit it.*

Last year, my parents traded in the old beige G3 for a new computer, and my 10-year-old brother started using the camera for his own wacky ends. My equip-

ment was disappearing. Even so, I think I'm ready to upgrade. I know that I will always keep my analog aesthetic. And when nobody remembers what it was like before digital video, the sounds of Django and Miles will ring in my ears, and I will remember what it was like to make something grainy, gritty, and real.

This author was accepted to the University of Chicago; his essay, about his evolution as a filmmaker, was undoubtedly a positive force in his application.

This piece has almost everything we look for in an effective application essay. We're shown that the author has passion in a particular field, and has pursued that passion aggressively and with some success. We learn something interesting about the author that probably wasn't entirely revealed in the rest of the application. This essay is also very interesting, which never hurts. The reader can't help but learn a little about filmmaking—not only technically, but also how a young filmmaker views his craft.

Far more than the previous two essays, this author focuses on the substance of what he's accomplished in a particular area.

Lessons to take away from this essay:

1. Your best essay subject, not surprisingly, is often the one thing you love to do and are most passionate about.

Can you imagine this author writing his essay, not about filmmaking, but about some vacation experience or sports accomplishment he had? It sounds preposterous—not because those would necessarily make poor essays, but because filmmaking is such an integral part of his life.

Not only does your "#1 activity" give you something to write about and show the admissions committees where you've chosen to focus your time, but it also frequently provides the fuel necessary for *you* to do your best writing. Isn't it easier to write about something when you're actually excited about what you're describing?

When students write essays about the activities they've chosen to pursue, those essays are often infused with an excitement and a passion that's contagious. If you have the opportunity to write such an essay, you should think twice about discarding it in favor of something else.

2. Details provide credibility.

In our experience, one couldn't do a much better job than this author in putting together a college admissions essay about filmmaking experiences. To be good, your essay doesn't need to be nearly this complete or full of expert reflection and analysis. However, when writing about your experiences, details are crucial. Details are essential to the telling of an interesting story—perhaps more importantly, they help convince the reader that you've had real-world experiences and that you're not inflating the importance of something for the purpose of the essay.

Too frequently, we read an essay from a student about, say, his love of travel. It turns out, though, that the essay is in actuality based upon a few trips to Europe. The student (often spurred by parents) has determined that this is his or her most "impressive" accomplishment to date. The essay is invariably dull because there's no real evidence that the student enjoys travel or has gained measurably from his experiences abroad. It's lacking *details*—descriptions of experiences or observations that would buttress the author's claim of being passionate about traveling.

Similarly, we also read a lot of essays about charity work that are long on platitudes ("It felt good to help the less fortunate" or "The look on their faces made it all worthwhile") and short on credible details about what the author did to help or how the experience made an impression on her. That's because, usually, the author did *little* to help (served soup five times) and it *didn't* really make much of an impression.

When you can write about such specifics as analog, digital, Django, film festivals, and temperamental editing software, your essay takes on an aura of authenticity that's especially valuable. By providing these details, you *prove* that you've put time and energy into whatever it is that you're writing about. Write about something in a way that *no one else could.*

Essay #4

I, Me, She, Her...Meredith

It is she, number 8971, senior graduating class, who you have met already. Her numbers fill the first pages of this application, these numbers which she uses to quantify and thus represent herself. Her 4.0's and 1480's and 6's establish her identity to the world: she exists purely in the universe of quantification.

She and I are very often confused, although upon glance we seem so very different. She is the intellectual, the academic reputation. She is classified through a series of numbers, while I am only understood through words. I adore poetry, popcorn, and playing tennis in the rain, and while she enjoys these endeavors, she prefers questioning and reasoning. At one time, I claimed she stifled me and tried to push her away, to send her numbers and her analytical questions to some other person, but she kept returning. At the time, I couldn't find a way to make us fit together: to ensure that her scholarly nature wouldn't overtake me. I wanted to be the dominant one, the one people invited places and wanted to see. Because of her intellect, I was being classified into a group I didn't belong in. She was the student, but I was more than that. I was talkative, artsy-crafty, energetic. But because she was in the honors' classes, she was all anyone could see: the one with the impressive numbers. I was being ignored. Yet as hard as I tried to rid myself of the intellect, the curiosity, she returned in full force. I couldn't escape it: she was still there. Gradually, we have become friends. I have begun to appreciate her as a companion; and while at times we hide in one another's shadows, we are now able to work in much more harmony than before: we are teammates with the same goal.

She is the tutor, the aspiring doctor, the perfectionist whose hands shake when public speaking. I am the pianist, the one who fills journals with unspoken words, and the one who starts philosophical arguments over the dinner table. I work comfortably within the universe of creativity and words, while she finds solace in the boundaries of logic and mathematics. Her thought process follows all logic and reason; I search for emotional and moral connections. I am impulsive, irrational, creative; she is sensible. And yet many times I am seen as only her.

Are we really all that different? Every day she and I are more and more intertwined with one another. Our drives match up perfectly; we have the same mantra: adversity is not an adequate deterrent. Each day we draw upon one another's source of energy, the other's inexplicable passion for life and learning, especially finding out the "Why" in everything. Every day, she gives me a little of her scholarly attitude, and every day I release to her a little of my creative spirit. She possesses the adoration of mathematics and science, establishes new ideas, and she also has the drive to succeed in what she takes on. I possess the builder's hands, the mechanism for the ideas to spur to life, to take form and succeed in themselves. We work together, we are friends, partners. We are both scholars, both "creative geniuses," over-zealous and outgoing, diligent and driven. Twisted and tangled, we are both Meredith, but one person, just one personality. She is I, I am she, and we are Meredith.

This essay is special because it reveals the author to be a complex individual—academically qualified, but also struggling with the burdens that the academic "grind" imposes upon a maturing young woman. Many smart kids feel the struggle Meredith describes between "she" and "I"; few, however, express it so articulately.

While Meredith's talent in describing how she's come to terms with her two disparate halves is the highlight of this essay, it also has several other strengths. The essay's format provides a forum for Meredith to describe some of her passions and interests, and to personalize her a little bit for the admissions committees (notice how she, almost in passing, mentions her plans to become a doctor). And the whole she/I/Meredith construction enables a literary approach that—while not perfect—demonstrates the author as a gifted writer not afraid to take risks with her prose.

Not surprisingly, Meredith was admitted Early Action to Harvard.

Lessons to take away from this essay:

1. Colleges like interesting people.

In our opinion, this essay is interesting to read. But perhaps even more importantly, it reveals an interesting person. Given the choice between a hard-working academic grind and the person described in this essay, any admissions officer would (all else being equal) choose this girl. She sounds fun. She's creative, "artsy craftsy," and argumentative.

She's also come to terms with her academic side and the intellectual pursuits that that part of her personality craves. This is not a nerd-become-rebel who has decided to shun the "uncool" fields of math and science. Rather, Meredith is a well-rounded high school senior with myriad interests and accomplishments.

She is someone who would add to the vitality of any college's freshman class.

2. It's possible to be philosophical and still write an effective admissions essay, but it's tough.

With this lesson we urge the utmost caution: for every successful "philosophical" essay, the college admissions landscape is littered with dozens of meandering, incomprehensible such essays that just don't work. The problem, to be blunt, is that 17-year olds don't usually have much to say about life in general that admissions officers haven't heard before. In fact, applicants usually sound better when they acknowledge that they *don't* already know everything there is to know about the world. As Socrates said: "The wise admits he knows nothing."

This author avoids that trap by explaining her own personal issues without claiming too much wisdom about life. This essay is about *her*, and about letting the admissions committees get to know her a little bit better.

Essay #5

It stands in the corner of a small room, gleaming in all its beauty, waiting for attention. Its silence resonates. During my childhood, it remained the exhibit devoid of touch, existing solely for my eyes. I struggled to resist my urge to tarnish its innocent magnificence with a cacophonous exposure. The day I finally sliced the thick silence, the sounds were devoured by the ravenous air and I thought I would never take my fingers off it again; I had finally struck the ivory of the grand piano.

Ever since that moment, I have wanted to learn everything about music and the majestic instrument I loved. I became the student of two piano teachers and a member of the National Fraternity of Student Musicians for four years. However, despite my interest and growing dedication, it became difficult to play the piano with an increasingly rigorous course-load every year at school. My usual practice sessions were burdened by excessive homework and other activities. Nevertheless, as a conscientious student of both music and high school, I developed a work ethic that allowed me to arrange my schedule making time for not only the things I had to do but also the things I loved to do.

As I am preparing for an audition to become a member of the National Guild of Piano Teachers, my playing has evolved. It has become more than a curiosity or a pastime; it is an escape. Mozart's "Sonata" soothes a stressful day of school; Gershwin's "Rhapsody in Blue" relives a magical outing; Chopin's "Nocturne" heals the bitter wounds left from an argument with a friend. Year after year the legatos of my music have complimented the staccatos of my life—a fantasia of memories. The piano exists as a source of companionship; a sentient with a pulse that throbs with emotion. The most rewarding experience of my life was breaking the silence that once existed in my home and beginning my endeavor into classical piano. I discovered my own soul through music.

This is another essay that "worked" at Harvard.

The author has written a short piece, and the choice of topic—while not unusual—doesn't fit exactly with what we usually preach. Playing a musical instrument, even at instructor-caliber, is impressive but not unique among Ivy League applicants. And there's no talk (at least in the essay) of piano-related accomplishments that might put this author in a class above her peers.

On the other hand, despite a few minor issues, this essay is written beautifully. Some parts are brilliant. Sure, anyone could assert a love for the piano. But reading this essay, do you have any doubt that this author is telling the truth—that she does, in fact, feel she has "discovered [her] own soul through music?"

While sending only this essay to a college might represent a missed opportunity in today's world of hyper-achieving high school seniors, as part of a comprehensive admissions package—including several diverse essays—it would do a terrific job of rounding out an application.

While a talked-about trend in the admissions committee is the "well-rounded class" as opposed to the "well-rounded student"—that is, a preference for people who do one thing excellently over those who do a number of things well—admissions officers are nonetheless looking for individuals who have a life and a self-awareness beyond academic studies and extracurricular, resume-building pursuits. This author's love of the piano, and the instrument's importance in her life, demonstrate that she is not a one-dimensional applicant, and that she takes joy and comfort in her art.

Lessons to take away from this essay:

If you're going to write passionately about something "ordinary," you need to make the essay work.

When you write an admissions essay about an amazing accomplishment or truly unique experience, your subject matter can sometimes stand on its own. That's not to say that you don't need to write a good essay. But just as Arnold Schwartzenegger can get away with a few less-than-stellar sequences in an action film (or stump speech), an essay about feeding starving children in Africa will always score at least *a few* points.

However, we've read some terrible essays about playing instruments, running, cooking, playing chess, knitting, and many other pastimes. That's because it's very difficult to make an essay about a common leisure activity interesting. It's also tricky to make it "about you," as opposed to something that could have been written by anyone.

It turns out that almost everyone who writes about running describes the meditative nature of jogging alone on a quiet trail. Those who love sailing write about being on the open water and knowing all about the boats, knots, and sails. Applicants who love to read talk about curling up with old friends such as Elizabeth from *Pride and Prejudice*. For admissions officers who read thousands of essays each year, it's hard to provide something of this nature that will make you sound interesting and provide any meaningful information about who you are. Sure, running is an integral part of your life. But that doesn't mean it necessarily deserves a prominent place in your college application. Remember, your job here is to impress and create a personal bond with the reader.

This essay is about playing the piano—something that literally millions of Americans do. But the importance of the piano to this applicant truly comes across in this special essay. Not only do we get the impression that this is an expert piano player, but we are also introduced to a young child who once yearned to play the grown-up instrument, and has now made it a stabilizing influence in her stressful and exciting life. What makes this essay work? Certainly the emotive language helps, and the inclusion of details lends credibility to the author's story. In the end, though, it *just works*; this essay *adds* to the application of which it is a part. By the time we are visualizing the author gratefully banging out Chopin upon the grand piano after a hard day, we know her better than we would have otherwise, and we probably like her more as well.

2. It's the message that matters.

This extremely well-written essay has a few awkward spots. Nonetheless, it's often beautiful, and the images painted by the author are memorable: the young girl looking up at the forbidden grand piano, and finally attacking it like a starving man on a loaf of bread; the overworked student relaxing with her instrument after a hard day; the reflective college applicant realizing the importance of the piano in helping her deal with the "staccatos" of her life.

The substance of and impression left by your essay matters more than verb conjugation or literary allusions. Admissions officers admit real people, and they want to connect with those people. The essay is not simply a writing test, and should not be treated as such.

Essay #6

Moving to a different country at the age of six was as much of an adventure for me as it was unmitigated torture for my mother. On a voyage that took more than twenty-four hours, the eager, wide eyes of my twin sister and I had not fluttered shut once—and neither had my mother's. At one o'clock in the morning, we squealed and fought for a glimpse out the plane's tiny window, as my exhausted mother apologized continuously to the sleep-deprived passengers. After eleven years, I still remember peeping out and gasping, gazing upon the bright lights of Los Angeles. A million specks of color, each one brilliant and full of possibilities lay beneath my feet. I was coming upon a country full of stars, and according to my mother, it was to be my new country; I could not tear my eyes away.

The first year of my new life in America was a year of firsts. It was the first time I had ever run under a sky so stunningly clear and blue, and so impossibly huge; it was the first time I had played with my sister in our own yard (with grass in it!), and not seen one skyscraper, it was the very first year I held in my chubby hands, the cold, white, amazing substance that is snow; and it was the first year that I fell in love with America.

That love has stayed with me through all the alienation that I have felt in this beautiful country, an alienation I became familiar with as early as elementary school. One day the counselor took my sister and I aside. "Girls," she said, "you are not required to recite the pledge of allegiance with the rest of the class. You may remain sitting." Although I continued to pledge my daily allegiance to the country that I love, a nagging voice always said, "Sit down. Your pledge means nothing. You're not 'required' to recite it." Was my mother right? Will this star-studded country ever let it be mine?

In school, I worked incessantly and passionately—maybe if I just worked hard enough, I would finally be accepted. Not until I was at the top, and better than anyone else, I believed, would I be good enough to be part of this country. So when I was given second chair of the flute section my seventh grade year, I burst into tears of disappointment. As usual, however, the tears quickly dried, allowing the cold-steeled determination in my inner core to shine through. I would just have to try harder and prove to America that I am worthy of its acceptance—and work harder I did. I easily auditioned my way to first chair second semester, and three years later, I was accepted in the All-State Honor Band. When I received an unacceptable B+ on my math test, I skipped tears altogether, and moved on to the determination stage. My days, already filled to the brim with music lessons, cross country, community service, band, and school, threatened to overflow, but my determination, strengthened by all the obstacles I had to overcome, held firm, and I increased my study time, forgoing sleep, food, and friends. I ended the year with the highest grade in all my core class. I tested into Central Academy (a school for gifted and talented students) the next year, and have taken advanced courses there ever since. Even at Central, however, I could not be anything less but at the top of my class.

Alas, however hard I worked, however much my body was drained from exhaustion, my mind weary from lack of sleep, I could not seem to gain ground in my race to be accepted. How can I, when I am labeled an "alien"; when I peer into the mirror and see a strange girl, with slanted eyes, yellow skin, and a flat nose starring back? She is utterly different from the beautiful large-eyed girls with rosy complexions that surround me everyday.

Feeling ostracized, I returned to my native country a few years ago, where my mother's roots are, and where I had been too young to leave mine. I do not think I have to say the hope that was in my heart…but I was disappointed. The faces of my relatives crowed around me, unfamiliar and foreign. My mind, indulged with open skies and wide spaces, rebelled against the crowded streets and soot covered skies of Taiwan. This too, then, was not were I belonged. At that moment, I felt lost—like a dandelion seed in a wild, relentless wind, tossed from one place to another, never to settle down.

Now, in my room, with a Chinese painting on one wall, and a Beatles poster on the other, I stare at my college applications: international student is checked, government financial aid is not. I am all alone. I look out my window, and through my tears, street lamps, lighted windows, and Christmas lights blur into the panorama of stars that called to me in my first glimpse of America. I will belong here some day, I promise. In this land where wishes come true, maybe the wild wind will stop, just for a while, and give me time to grow my roots.

This beautifully-written essay is different and unique. It's an immigrant's story of coming to America, and her ongoing struggle to fit in here.

Lesson to take away from this essay:

If honest and not manipulated, emotional prose can have a powerful effect on an application.

To us, this essay is stunning: while poetic and evocative, it also resonates with the innocent longing of a teenaged girl. We won't describe *why* we found the images, metaphors, and succinctly expressed thoughts of this author so powerful, but we urge you to read through the essay again. What does it make you feel? Can you sympathize with this girl's plight? If you were an admissions committee member, how would this essay interact with the test scores and grades you already had for this applicant?

One of the primary goals of your essay is to humanize you for the admissions committee. The essay isn't just for evaluating how well you can write; rather, it's your opportunity to show the committee who you are, what's important to you, and what makes you tick. If you can help the reader to empathize with an emotion you feel deeply—here, a desire to thrive in an environment where the author feels like an outsider—then you can *move* the reader into knowing you *as a person*, rather than a set of numbers and data on a page.

In the best of worlds, you can encourage the reader to actually get behind you and take up your cause (in the case of an admissions officer, to recommend you to the rest of the committee). Just like the underdog at the end of a good movie, the author of the above essay likely has most readers rooting for her to succeed—to finally grasp, through admission to a prestigious college and perhaps financial aid, the elusive American Dream.

Essay #7

Kurt and Me

I am not Vonnegut. He is not me. I did not fight in World War Two. He did not break his arm in the third grade. We are separate people, yet under the light of the literary world we are bonded together—he as an author, and I as a reader. Our relationship began in 1996 when I first read his novel <u>Welcome to the Monkey House</u>. Sure we had a good time, but it wasn't love. Over the past 5 years our affair has burgeoned with unbridled passion. Today, I stand completely devoted, respectful and honored to have my place with Vonnegut. I am a reader.

As a lowly pre-teen with no passion for myself, let alone others, I had a shallow relationship with Kurt. We were two strangers at a party, discussing the weather while piling bite size nachos, cookies, and carrots onto our designer napkins. I was intrigued by Vonnegut's words; I enjoyed his stories for their simplicity and their sweetness. They were my punch to wash down the dry cookies.

Kurt gave me a gift that served to form the base of our relationship. He taught that my writing mattered. His simply constructed sentences and straightforward plots gave me hope; my subject matters could be interesting also. I felt that my sentences, even though not splattered with adjectives and copious description, could be meaningful. I did not lose faith despite the low quality of my work. I knew I could get better, that there could be meaning inside of my words.

Through more schooling I did eventually betray Kurt. I became a mistress to the semicolon, a slave to the adjective. I found myself new lovers. John Steinbeck taught me description. Ayn Rand gave me long sentences with hints of sarcasm. I matured after my relationship with Kurt, but soon found myself yearning to rekindle the old flame. So I did. This was no puppy love. We exploded in passion, I read and absorbed Kurt's words as if they were written especially for me. His philosophies, his conceptions about the American culture were filled with simple truths.

In <u>God Bless You, Mr. Rosewater</u>, the main character has a simple maxim: "God damn it, you've got to be kind." These eight words—twenty-seven letters—sum up a large part of Vonnegut's humanist viewpoints. There is no moral more fundamental than human kindness.

When stress rules one's life, one often acts irrationally, taking on the qualities of an irritable individual. About a month ago, I was very over-worked, over-stressed, and under-slept while finishing up a school project. Many friends with whom I conversed that week were not pleased to have had the experience. And then the phrase lurked into the tightly balled fist of my mind. "God damn it, you've got to be kind." I realized that this adage holds true no matter what the circumstances. Tired or not, courtesy and friendliness should be top priority. The line has stuck close to my heart; it is a picture of Kurt to carry in my wallet.

We're married now, Kurt and I. The wild passion has tamed into deep love and respect. We stand by each other as author and reader. Vonnegut and his influ-

ences will forever be a part of me. I will be kind, I will respect my own writing, and I will dream. These I will wear as a wedding band, a symbol of permanence. We are a couple, however I have not remained completely devoted. My adjectives, my semicolons, my circumlocution are all vices; arguments vibrating through the ornately decorated walls of the white picket-fenced home. But I am not Kurt. Kurt is not me. We are each individuals, forever learning and redefining ourselves. We are simply together, author and reader.

This MIT student loves literature, and it shows. Ordinarily, topics such as this one make the essay-writing process difficult, as it's hard to write something unique about an activity as ubiquitous as reading. For the most part, it's all been said before.

However, this author takes a unique approach. Not only does she give the reader a great deal of information about herself as she describes her interest—she was once a "lowly pre-teen with no passion for [her]self"; as a young writer she was encouraged to know she could express herself without a large vocabulary; she cherishes kindness—but she uses an interesting device in comparing her relationship with the author Kurt Vonnegut to a romantic one. While this device isn't perfect and is even a little awkward in places, it's a daring and impressive technique for a young writer. It also works—this author views her experiences with Vonnegut's as incredibly important, and she's able to convey that importance through this approach.

Lessons to take away from this essay:

1. When writing about a passion, provide details about yourself and how you've been impacted.

Many people write about their love of reading. Such essays generally fail—not because reading is an inherently unsuitable topic, but because the applicants don't reveal anything interesting about themselves or how their experiences have been unique.

To say that you love to curl up with a good book, and to see the characters come alive in your head, merely puts you in the group of tens of millions of Americans who enjoy fiction. To say something worthy of a college application—a forum designed to help you convey a sense of yourself to a competitive school—you need to go beyond the ordinary and pull something special from your own experiences. As this author put it, "we were two strangers at a party, discussing the weather while piling bite size nachos, cookies, and carrots onto our designer napkins." For many people this type of insight just isn't possible, and so they wisely choose another topic.

This author is also a writer, and she discusses details of her reading history that help us understand her relationship with the activity. She initially enjoyed reading Vonnegut as an easy and fun leisure activity. She later learned to appreciate authors with more complex writing styles, but also returned to Vonnegut and his "simple truths." While we think the author could have included even more details, she definitely does a good job of *showing* (remember your writing teacher saying "show, don't tell"?) how Vonnegut impacted her life and why she finds her relationship with his writing so important.

2. One of the most impressive things you can do in an admissions essay is show growth and development.

While colleges obviously want to admit smart and impressive kids, one of the most crucial qualities they seek in applicants is self-awareness and the ability to grow, improve, and learn from mistakes. Colleges often see themselves as laboratories that encourage and nurture developing minds, and as a result they're far more interested in who you'll become than what you've been in the past. That's why, for example, so many schools will look positively at an upward grade trend, even when freshman and sophomore grades (and thus average GPA) are significantly lower.

Great college essays frequently demonstrate that the applicant has learned from life, and that he or she has an active mind that is seeking out new experiences and new ways to grow. A "standard" essay about reading might describe learning to read as a young child, and continuing with that interest through young adulthood. However, this applicant makes clear that she not only reads, but has considered the impact of that interest—and particularly of one author—on her reading, writing, and worldview. Vonnegut taught her that she could write meaningfully at a young age despite a limited command of vocabulary and literary maturity. She later learned to enjoy and adopt more sophisticated writing and storytelling techniques from other authors. She's gleaned philosophical lessons from Vonnegut. Finally, after all of these experiences, she's acknowledged that she is "forever learning" as a reader.

For colleges, finding that person who is "forever learning" and re-examining herself is of the utmost importance. By showing not just what you've done, but also how you've been affected by that experience and what you've learned from it, you can demonstrate yourself to be someone who will continue to grow and thrive in a college setting.

978-0-595-35582-2
0-595-35582-X

Printed in the United States
30500LVS00005B/109-114

9 780595 355822